To Rosemary

From Writing to Computers

We do not need to look far for signs of divided consciousness with regard to books and computers. For instance, the United Kingdom Data Protection Act 1984 gave British subjects some rights of access to computer-held information on themselves but not to paper records. *From Writing to Computers* takes as its central theme the issue of a unifying intellectual principle to connect books and computers.

Julian Warner uses an approach based on semiotics, and also draws on linguistics, information science, cognitive science, philosophy and automata studies. Covering a range of topics from the relations between speech and writing to transitions from orality to literacy and claims for a transition to an information society, the author aims throughout to render complex ideas intelligible without loss of rigour.

From Writing to Computers addresses ordinary readers who, as social beings and members of political communities, are affected by, and implicated in, significant developments in methods for storing, manipulating and communicating information. It is also intended for students of the disciplines on which the book draws: semiotics, information studies, linguistics, computer science, philosophy and psychology.

The author of a number of articles in librarianship and information science, **Julian Warner** is Lecturer in the Information Management Division at the Queen's University of Belfast.

From Writing to Computers

Julian Warner

London and New York

First published 1994
by Routledge
11 New Fetter Lane, London EC4P 4EE

Simultaneously published in the USA and Canada
by Routledge
29 West 35th Street, New York, NY 10001

Typeset in Palatino by LaserScript, Mitcham, Surrey
Printed and bound in Great Britain by
Biddles Ltd, Guildford and King's Lynn

British Library Cataloguing in Publication Data
A catalogue record for this book is available from the British Library

Library of Congress Cataloging in Publication Data
Warner, Julian, 1955–
  From writing to computers / Julian Warner.q
  p. cm.
  Includes bibliographical references (p.) and index.
  1. Computers. 2. Creative writing. I. Title.
  QA76.W239 1994   93–32312
  302.2–dc20   CIP

ISBN 0–415–09612–X

'A little redness, or a little matter of Bone, here or there, what does it signify to Me?'

I sagaciously observed, if it didn't signify to him, to whom did it signify?

(Dickens, *Great Expectations*, 1861: 47)

Contents

Figures

Acknowledgements

I would like to thank Aslib: the Association for Information Management for permission to adapt articles first published by them.

Chapter 1: 'Semiotics' was adapted from: 'Semiotics, information science, documents and computers', *Journal of Documentation*, 46 (1), 1990, pp. 16–32.

Chapter 2: 'Writing' was developed from: 'Writing, programs, computers and logic', in: Kevin P. Jones (ed.), *Informatics 11: The Structuring of Information* (Proceedings of a conference held at the University of York, 20–22 March 1991), London: Aslib, 1991, pp. 109–45.

Part of Chapter 3: 'Intelligence of documents' and the substance of Chapter 5: 'Intelligence of computers' were derived from: 'A note on the literal intelligence of computers and documents', *Journal of Documentation*, 47 (2), 1991, pp. 163–90.

Doubleday granted permission to reproduce an extract from: Homer, *The Iliad*, trans. R. Fitzgerald and intr. G.S. Kirk, Oxford: Oxford University Press, 1984.

I would like to record my debts to the following readers who read the manuscript, or precursors to and portions of it, and criticized and encouraged: Pamela Clayton, Sabina Jones, Michael Buckland, Patrick Wilson, Judy Weedman, Clifford Lynch, and, for a particularly detailed and scrupulous reading, the anonymous publisher's reader.

Author's note

Dates given by references to items without known publication dates, such as dialogues by Plato, reflect approximate absolute datings and generally agreed relative chronological order, but are not intended as contributions to scholarly debates about absolute or relative dates.

Some logical symbols are introduced in the text. These include:

∧   and
∨   or
~   not
→   If . . . then
↔   If, and only if, . . . then
| Sheffer stroke (see p. 104 for a reading)
∃   There exists
φ   Greek phi

These logical symbols can be given verbal correlates, as indicated. However, these verbal readings should be understood as informal renderings which may initially aid understanding and not as final or precise interpretations.

Introduction

Various collocations of symbols become familiar as representing important collocations of ideas; and in turn the possible relations – according to the rules of the symbolism – between these collocations of symbols become familiar, and these further collocations represent still more complicated relations between the abstract ideas. And thus the mind is finally led to construct trains of reasoning in regions of thought in which the imagination would be entirely unable to sustain itself without symbolic help.

(Whitehead and Russell 1913: 2)

Signs of divided consciousness with regard to documents and computers are apparent. For instance, the United Kingdom Data Protection Act 1984 gave British subjects some rights of access to computer-held information on themselves but not to paper records (Data Protection Act 1984). Some commentators expressed disquiet at this division in rights of access to significant information. A full and persuasive expression of concern was made by D.F. McKenzie in the 1985 Panizzi lectures: 'one might feel that some central, unifying concept of "the text" had broken down'. Panizzi, the nineteenth-century librarian who transformed the British Museum Library into an institution of national, and international, significance partly by his insistence on the full collection of documents published within the political regions governed by the United Kingdom, would have been disturbed at this loss of unity and would not

have simply accepted computing as just another technological aid, one more efficient than others for doing certain jobs . . . [but] would have asked: on what unifying, intellectual principle, does it relate to books?

(McKenzie 1986: 42–3)

The significance of such a consideration should not require undue insistence. The issue of a 'unifying, intellectual principle' to connect books and computers forms the central theme for this book.

The theme helps to delineate the intended readership. Citizens of social and political communities are implicated in significant changes in methods for storing, manipulating and communicating information. In the words of a position traceable to Aristotle, a human being is 'by nature a political animal'. A citizen can make a deliberate choice to become asocial, but only by denying full humanity: 'Any one who by his nature and not simply by ill-luck has no state is either too bad or too good, either subhuman or superhuman' (Aristotle 323 BCc: 59). The book, then, is addressed to ordinary readers who, as social beings, are affected by developments in information technologies.

Other, more narrowly academic, signs of divided consciousness with regard to books and computers can be detected and these indicate a second broad category of intended reader. For instance, within the uncertain and mutable boundaries of information studies, differentiations between fields tend to be made partly on the basis of alignments with particular media for information storage or retrieval, with a broad spectrum from manuscripts, through printed documents and audio-visual materials, to computers (Warner 1990). At the same time, boundaries between disciplines are changing and breaking down under the pervasive influence of information technology. This text draws on semiotics (or the study of systems of signs), linguistics, information science, cognitive science, logic, philosophy and automata studies. It may be of reciprocal interest to specialists from those disciplines. Specialists are also inescapably members of political communities. The book, then, is addressed to students, at all levels, from those disciplines and to those specialists in their capacity as members of broader political communities.

A number of perspectives on the computer have been explicitly formulated and some of the more significant can be indicated here. Analogies between the computer and the human brain or mind have been pervasive and have emerged in a variety of forms. For example, on one important interpretation, cognitive science demands that 'theories of the mind should be expressed in a form that can be modelled in a computer program', without recourse to intuition (Johnson-Laird 1988: 52). A recent, and significant, contribution to linguistics, itself indebted to cognitive science, *Relevance: Communication and Cognition* models the mind, and comprehension of utterances, as a formal system or automaton (Sperber and Wilson 1986: 94). Research into neural networks which, on one account (Ford 1989), aims to simulate the parallel processing characteristic of human brain processes also rests on an extensive analogy between computational and human intellectual processes.

In other discussions, the computer is either left unplaced with regard to other information technologies or characterized as a 'radical novelty' (Dijkstra 1989): an appearance of explanation which is not an explanation. It is now time to begin to situate the computer in relation to other information technologies, including writing. The perspective to be established marks a subtle, although still radical, departure from analogies between the computer and human brain or mind.

The treatment of the topics to be discussed here has been influenced by semiotics and this carries implications for the approach to definitions of terms. A theme of semiotics is that definitions are finally circular and reciprocal unless a residue of undefined terms is left. Concise definitions can therefore only indicate the sense of a term, not exhaust its scope. Analogously, for Kuhn in *The Structure of Scientific Revolutions*, verbal definitions were aids to understanding, not complete specifications of meaning, if such were possible. Scientific concepts could only obtain full significance when systematically related to other concepts within the paradigm. Concepts fundamental to a particular scientific paradigm may be impossible to define within that paradigm (Kuhn 1962). Even if precise definitions of some terms can be established, there may be problems in assigning objects of discourse to agreed categories: for instance, the distinction between what is to be regarded as part of a program and what as data can become arbitrary.

Indications of the sense of terms, not to be confused with final definitions, can still be given. This will be attempted when complex, or potentially unfamiliar, terms are introduced. Some terms are deliberately treated as largely primitive, as open to elucidation and description, but not amenable to final definition. Significant terms treated as largely primitive in the subsequent discourse include 'intelligence', 'writing' and the 'semiotic faculty'. Even where a term is taken as beyond final definition, different senses can be distinguished: for instance, the appearance of intelligence can be contrasted with the substance of intelligence, to be denoted by the qualification '*literal* intelligence'. With these reservations in mind, the structure and themes of the book can be prefigured.

SEMIOTICS

Semiotics regards sign systems, such as speech and writing, as products of a unified faculty for constructing socially shared systems of signs. It also provides a source for subtle and incisive distinctions between aspects of the sign and between types of sign. Particular attention is given to the differentiation of signifier, sign and signified. Expression and content, form and meaning, are seen to convey a distinction analogous to that of signifier from signified, with signs corresponding to the relation made between the two terms in the process of interpretation. Distinctions established are then used to bring documents and computers within the single analytical category of the signifier.

WRITING

This chapter considers the complex relation between writing and speech. Classic discussions of language tended to regard written language as a secondary system of signs, whose only purpose was to represent spoken language. More recently, the relative autonomy of speech and of writing as systems of signs has been emphasized. A series of contrasts between written and spoken language, none of which amounts to an absolute difference, is then indicated. Writing apparently intended primarily for preservation of information over time can also be distinguished from writing intended for the transmission of messages over space as well as the preservation of information over time. Recognition of contrasts between written and spoken language enables a subtle position to be developed: that one form of writing, exemplified by alphabetic written language, draws on models in oral discourse, but that a strong connection with speech is not necessary for graphic signification to be regarded as writing. Programming can then be recognized as a form of writing not apparently intended as a communicative substitute for speech.

INTELLIGENCE OF DOCUMENTS

A dialogue by Plato, the *Phaedrus*, has emerged as a crucial text for an understanding of the transition from orality to literacy in Ancient Greece. Anxieties associated with the introduction of written language to primarily oral societies are considered, with examples drawn from the Greek world and other contexts. The dialogue itself is then placed in its historical context, with particular attention to the development of logical forms of enquiry and argument. The contrasts made by Plato between speech and writing in the *Phaedrus*, and the attribution there of intelligence to publicly circulated documents in written language, are discussed.

COMPUTERS

On the interpretation of writing established – that a connection with models in oral discourse is not necessary for graphic signification to be regarded as writing – a computer program has been recognized as a written artefact. An account of the logical operations associated with the computer is also required, for the sake of completeness. Yet the complexity and variety of programming languages threatens to frustrate the possibility of providing such an account. Automata theory provides models for programs, data and the computer which enable an enquirer to avoid real-world problems over the definition of these terms. An account of the main themes of automata theory is given, together with an indication of its possible integration with formal logic. The schema which correlates the models developed in automata theory with real-world programs, data and computers is indicated too. The semiotic aspects of models of the computational process, particularly the crucial role of graphic representation in enabling the constructions of elaborate models and processes, are also considered.

INTELLIGENCE OF COMPUTERS

Claims for the literal intelligence of computers can be regarded as one aspect of the pervasive analogies between the computer and human brain or mind. The Turing test, published by Alan Turing in 1950, was made significant by its adoption by some subsequent research. It involved the simulation of convincing human linguistic responses to questions. The development of claims for the intelligence of computers is traced from their origin in the post-1945 intellectual and political context to their refutation by Searle in 1980, at a point when computers were being increasingly assimilated into wider social life outside specialized research communities.

CONCLUSION

The development of the form of writing represented by computer programming seems partly to have enabled a reassessment of the relation between writing and speech. Changes in consciousness have tended to lag behind the technical developments which partly motivated them. Spoken and written language, and other forms of writing, can be regarded as products of the semiotic faculty for constructing systems of signs. Linguistics has reiterated the proposition that there are no primitive spoken languages, in the sense that societies have developed languages sufficient to meet their communicational needs. Recognition of a unified semiotic faculty seems to legitimate an extension of this proposition to other sign systems, including writing: that, subject to delays, societies develop methods for storing and communicating information sufficient to meet their needs.

Comprehending such a range of topics requires the integration of issues usually considered separately. Yet inherited disciplinary boundaries are not adequate to deal with the challenge of establishing a 'unifying, intellectual principle' for books and computers. The approach here rests on similar grounds to Huckleberry Finn's preference for pot-cooking over food prepared as separate items:

> When you got to the table you couldn't go right to eating, but you had to wait for the widow to tuck down her head and grumble a little over the victuals, though there warn't really anything the matter with them. That is, nothing only everything was cooked by itself. In a barrel of odds and ends it is different; things get mixed up, and the juice kind of swaps around, and the things go better.
>
> (Twain 1884: 2)

The division of study into separate disciplines seems to be, although only in part, historically subsequent to the development of written language. A stress on divisions between disciplines, and some of the specific disciplines isolated, can be traced to the Aristotelian emphasis on mutually exclusive classifications (Goody and Watt 1963: 54). Yet boundaries between disciplines should not be taken for substantive distinctions between things in the world or objects of study. Even Leibniz, with his insistence on order and logic, testified to the 'mutual penetration and connexion of things' (Leibniz 1689: 111).

Once the liberty of combining topics often considered separately is conceded, there are problems posed by the specialized modes of discourse favoured, or demanded, by different disciplines. Saussure in the *Course in General Linguistics* noted that advanced stages of societies were associated with 'the development of certain special languages (legal language, scientific terminology, etc.)' (Saussure 1916: 21). Such languages may be partly or predominantly transmitted or received in written forms, rather than by oral interaction. Saussure's insistence that the spoken word alone constituted the object of study for linguistics (Saussure 1916: 24–5) may be a partial explanation for his failure fully to develop this particular insight. Yet other aspects of Saussurean linguistics can be used to elucidate the nature of such special languages: like dialects, they need only differ by degrees from one another, by an accumulation of contrasts, and need not occupy distinct spaces (Saussure 1916: 191–207). In the sociology of knowledge, it has been noted that pluralistic societies depart from a common language and that there may be competition between sub-universes of meaning (Berger and Luckmann 1966). Different languages are developed for different conceptual frameworks. With some aspects of special languages, such as the use of mathematical, logical or chemical symbolism, differences from other discourse are marked by their relatively extensive use of non-alphabetic forms. In other aspects, differences can be disguised by their use of terms from wider discourse in specialized senses (Davies 1987). For instance, in automata theory the term 'machine' is used to refer to a written expression and to the configuration of a computer. The aim here is to provide accessibility without loss of rigour and to write in an increasingly elusive common discourse. A progression from a relatively strict compliance with the formalities of each field of discourse to a degree of informality, legitimized by its more formal precursor, will be attempted.

Specialized languages, while they may be essential to the construction of elaborate conceptual structures, can also disguise or protect poverty of thought. For instance, economists have constructed elaborate schemas for describing and predicting economic activity (Roberts 1982). A sceptical observer of economics might question their predictive value, while acknowledging their internal coherence (Wilson 1983: 7–48). Consensus within a group can be distinguished from the legitimacy of a claim to cognitive authority over the chosen subjects of study of that group (Wilson 1983). While conceding that authority in a subject is inevitably a political construction, finally determined by the group which has the persuasive power to obtain control of the debate, patterns can be changed and have changed.

In this text, the emphasis will be on the significance of the exactness enabled by writing (Bacon 1597: 209). Yet it should not be forgotten that Bacon also observed, 'Conference [maketh] a ready man' (Bacon 1597: 209), and that scholarly communication can productively be regarded as a public conversation in print or other communicative media. The isolated document, even once published, cannot contribute to knowledge until it has been received, considered and assessed by members of the relevant discursive communities, either informally or publicly and formally (Wilson 1983). Let this contribution, then, be considered as a development of a dialogue which can be continued.

Finally, in treating a large topic within a compact space, Lytton Strachey's axiom has been taken as a guide:

> To preserve, for instance, a becoming brevity – a brevity which excludes everything that is redundant and nothing that is significant – that, surely, is the first duty of the biographer.
>
> (Strachey 1918: 10)

Lytton Strachey himself, appealed to as a precedent in an unfamiliar context, might have been further surprised to be informed that he had informally anticipated concepts central to the disciplines yoked together: redundancy to information theory; and significance to semiotics.

Chapter 1

Semiotics

And God said, Let there be lights in the firmament of the heaven to divide the day from the night; and let them be for signs, and for seasons, and for days, and years.

(Genesis 1.14)

INTRODUCTION

Semiotics, or semiology, tends to be formally defined as the study of systems of signs.[1] Saussure's proposal in the *Course in General Linguistics*, first published in 1916, that it was possible to conceive of a science, to be called semiology after the Greek *semeion* or sign, which would study *'the role of signs as part of social life'* (Saussure 1916: 15) has been taken as a seminal (Barthes 1984), if unfortunately exiguous (Harris 1987b: 26–32), impulse to the development of subsequent semiotics. Semiotics was to be distinguished from linguistics by its concern with all forms of signification rather than exclusively with spoken language. Spoken language was one among other social sign systems, such as written language, codes of gesture, military signals and the like, although, for Saussure, it was the most important. All social sign systems were regarded as the product of a single faculty: 'it is not spoken language which is natural to man, but the faculty of constructing a language, i.e. a system of distinct signs corresponding to distinct ideas' (Saussure 1916: 10). The idea of a single faculty concerned with creating order by constructing systems of signs yields a unifying principle for semiotics. Although it has sustained this unifying principle, semiotics remains a tentative (Barthes 1973; 1984: 77), internally complex, study, sometimes embarrassed by its scope and concerned to set boundaries to its investigation (Eco 1976; 1984).

A powerful analytical terminology for the study of signs has been developed. Aspects of the sign are differentiated. A sign is constituted by something standing for something else, by a relation between the thing signifying and the thing signified. Signifier, sign and signified are typically distinguished. Form and meaning, expression and content convey a distinction similar, although not identical, to that of signifier from signified. The trichotomy of signifier, sign and signified can yield a more sophisticated, incisive and discriminating way of enforcing differentiations between aspects of the sign than can be obtained from any other known source (Sturrock 1986: 14). Semiotics derives some further unity from its relatively consistent invocation of this triad. Its use for analytical purposes can also help establish connections between previously disparate subject areas. The distinction of signifier, sign and signified will be more fully described later in this chapter, when it is used to establish a common categorization of documents in written language and computer programs.

Different types of sign are also distinguished by semiotics. For instance, an index is indirect evidence of the object or event signified, with a causal relation to that object or event (Eco 1976: 115), such as the footprint found by Robinson Crusoe or wet ground after rain or dew. In the case of an icon, there is a resemblance between signifier and signified: Dürer's drawing of a rhinoceros is given as one example of an iconic sign (Eco 1976: 205). Graphic signs can be distinguished from phonic signs. Within the graphic, scriptorial signs, exemplified by alphabetic written language, can be contrasted with pictorial signs. Texts differ in the number and types of sign distinguished, with a degree of arbitrariness in choice in distinctions made, and in interpretations given to terms for types of sign. Changes in the meaning of one term will tend to affect the senses taken by other terms in the cluster (Barthes 1984: 101–4). These distinctions between types of sign will be valuable later in the argument in differentiating written from spoken language, and in contrasting the diagrammatic or iconic forms favoured for discussions of automata with the scriptorial signs associated with formal logic. In those contexts, relevant distinctions will be more fully elucidated.

The intention here is to use distinctions between aspects of the sign, between signifier, sign and signified, to indicate a unified view of documents and computers. Discussion of computer operations to date has tended to be in terms of symbol or token manipulation or information processing. From a semiotic perspective, written language, often represented by documents, is included, and computer programs can be comprehended, within the single category of the signifier, not the sign nor the signified. It should be noted, however, that this categorization of computer programs has not been established by those texts concerned with semiotics which also touch on, or discuss, information theory and cybernetics (Derrida 1976; Eco 1976; 1984; Barthes 1984; Poster 1990).

Let us begin by reviewing the terminology associated with computing, and noting its possible derivation from disciplinary contexts connected with the development of computing; follow this with a fuller account of the contrasts between signifier, sign and signified; and then bring computer programs, and data, within the analytical category of the signifier.

TERMINOLOGY OF COMPUTING

The discussion of computer operations in terms of symbol and token manipulation and information processing can be related to disciplinary contexts significant to the development of computing: symbol to symbolic logic; token also to logic; and information to information theory, concerned with the economic and accurate transmission of messages. In these disciplinary contexts, symbol, token and information are given precise, technical meanings. For instance, for Boole (Boole 1854: 6–25) a symbol was required to have an invariant meaning within a single process of reasoning. In logic, token can be used to denote a particular utterance or written occurrence of a linguistic expression. It is distinguished from an expression-type which is an abstract entity considered apart from potential or actual instantiations of the expression (Brody 1967). Information in *The Mathematical Theory of Communication* was a measure of freedom of choice when selecting a message from a source (Shannon and Weaver 1949: 6–30). Information was also clearly differentiated from meaning and 'the semantic aspects of communication were irrelevant to the engineering problem' (Shannon and Weaver 1949: 25).

Symbol, token and information were already present as terms in wider discourse, but with a wider range of meanings not similarly delimited by explicit, prescriptive definitions. Symbol does not necessarily denote an invariant entity and information is often connected with meaning. Their existence in ordinary discourse may explain the wide adoption of these terms to refer to computer operations. Ambiguities can result from a mixing of intra-disciplinary senses with meanings present and sustained in ordinary discourse. Most frequently the concept of information has been extended, sometimes without explicit notice, to include meaning. To some extent, confusion has been countered by an insistence that the information aspects can be meaningfully distinguished from the technical aspects of information technology (Laver 1983: 5; Roberts and Clarke 1987a; 1987b). However, as single, and rather isolated, terms, symbol, token and information do not offer the contrasts which can be obtained from the distinction of signifier, sign and signified.

SIGNIFIER, SIGN AND SIGNIFIED

An aspect of semiotics is a resistance to final definitions (Eco 1984: 44–68). A linguistic term obtains its meaning from its place in an indefinite network of slightly or greatly differing terms and its meaning is accordingly subject to change with alterations in the senses of other terms (Saussure 1916: 113). The senses of signifier, sign and signified are then chiefly given by their difference from each other as proximate terms. The distinction of signifier from signified can be both valuable and incisive, but can also lead to excessive abstraction and over-simplification if rigidly pursued (Derrida 1976).

Different contents can be given to the categories of signifier, sign and signified. In Saussure's *Course in General Linguistics* they are developed primarily in relation to spoken language (Saussure 1916), but they have since been applied to the analysis of other systems of signs such as written language, film and television. Other terms corresponding to the distinction of signifier, sign and signified have been proposed, such as expression, relation and content (Barthes 1984). They have not been as widely adopted and, although they can be useful in exposition, a degree of standardization is valuable for the connections it can imply or be made to yield.

Representation in graphic form may help to clarify the relation between signifier, sign and signified:

$$\text{Signifier} \quad \rightarrow \quad \text{Signified}$$
$$\text{Sign}$$

The signifier lies at the beginning of an act of signification. It is linked to the signified by a human subject, excluding, with the aim of analytical clarity, animal signification or zoosemiosis. The sign is formed by the act of uniting a signifier to a signified. Expression, relation and content can be shown in similar graphic form to signifier, sign and signified:

$$\text{Expression} \quad \rightarrow \quad \text{Content}$$
$$\text{Relation}$$

An expression is connected to a content, with the relation between expression and content existing in the interpreter's mind, while that connection is being made (Saussure 1916; Barthes 1973; 1984; Eco 1976; 1984).

Spoken language is one sign system which can be used to exemplify these distinctions. There the signifier would be the sound pattern uttered or heard and the signified the meaning attached to those uttered sounds. The sign is the whole, the union of sound pattern and concept, of signifier and signified:

$$\text{Sound pattern} \quad \rightarrow \quad \text{Concept}$$
$$\text{Signifier} \quad \rightarrow \quad \text{Signified}$$
$$\text{Sign}$$

It is the act of union of signifier and signified which creates the sign as an entity and the entity tends to dissolve if we concentrate only on the signifier. If we listen only to the sounds of spoken language we may lose the meaning. Spoken language is itself formed in the division of the amorphous masses of sound and thought by connection with each other. Neither sound patterns nor meanings have independent existences: a sound pattern is only differentiated from noise by its meaning, and meaning in spoken language can only exist with the support of some sound pattern (Saussure 1916: 67, 101, 110, 138).

Differences in emphasis emerge when signifier and signified are differentiated in written, rather than spoken, language. In written language, the signifier would be the sentence, phrase, word or other intentional graphic mark, the signified the meaning attached to that mark, and the sign the union of the two. The form of entry used in a monolingual dictionary, of defined word and definition, has been regarded as analogous to the distinction of signifier from signified (Harris 1980):

Defined word (signifier)	Definition (signified)
Web	Texture; anything woven (Johnson 1755a)

Even in the rather reified and static form given by a dictionary entry, the sign is not recorded on the page but is made by the connecting act of the reader. The cultural status of the mono-lingual dictionary has been advanced as one influence towards the acceptance of the value of the distinction of signifier from signified within linguistics (Harris 1980), but it can be a mis-leading model for sequential written language. Only the signifier is given in such a text whereas the signified is connected with the mental activity of the interpreter: 'the readers who sat here at these radiating lines of desks, what were they but hapless flies caught in a huge web, its nucleus the great circle of the Cata-logue?' (Gissing 1891).

Signifier	Signified
Web	Spider's web / connotations of the complexity of printed matter and of libraries

Interpretation is also more complex, resorting to inference, rather than the simpler act of linking equivalent terms implied by the dictionary entry. In this extract, inference from 'flies' is needed to give an appropriate signified to the signifier, with a reference to a spider's web implied. Connotations other than the complexity of printed matter and of libraries could also be adduced: there is an openness in interpretation rather than the delimitation suggested by a dictionary definition. Written language – the sign system represented, although not exclusively, by documents – then belongs to the category of the signifier.

Other sign systems can be comprehended by these analytical distinctions. In the case of a dream, the sign would be the act of dreaming; the contrast between signifier and signified can be discovered in the distinction between the remembered dream and its latent content, without priority being given to either term (Barthes 1973: 114). With a newspaper photograph, the signifier would be the photographic image and caption, the signified the meaning given to that image and caption, and the sign the union of image and caption with meaning (Hartley 1982; Barthes 1982). The semiotic categories of signifier, sign and signified can, then, be given different contents from different fields.

Distinctions established above can now be summarized. The signifier lies at the beginning of an act of signification and, in such an act, is linked to a signified by a human interpreter. Some substance, some material form, is essential to the signifier. The particular substance, whether sound patterns, chiselled inscriptions on stone, or print on paper, is not relevant at the first level of analysis. The signified is the product, rather than the beginning, of the act of signification and is connected with the mental activity of the interpreter. The sign is formed in the temporary union of signifier with signified. These distinctions, although deliberately pared down, are still sufficient to join computer programs with written language, in the single analytical category of the signifier.

A particular copy of a computer program or a file of machine-readable data are evidently material representations of information. A defining quality of the signifier was that it must have some external substance, had to be given some material expression. In contrast, the signified was connected with the mental activity of a human interpreter and the sign was only constituted by the union of signifier and signified. It should, then, be clear that both program and data can be brought within the category of the signifier.

CONCLUSION

Signifier, sign and signified are intended to be highly general categories. They are also more marginal to ordinary discourse than symbol, token or information. Even at the most abstract level they can be used to enforce distinctions, between form and meaning or between a material expression and human thought. Such distinctions are difficult to obtain, without repeated insistence, from a more isolated and multivalent term such as information.

Chapter 2

Writing

'I *tole* you I got a hairy breas', en what's de sign un it; en I *tole* you I ben rich wunst, en gwineter be rich *agin*; en it's come true; en heah she *is! Dah*, now! doan' talk to *me* – signs is *signs*' ... Tom's most well, now, and got his bullet around his neck on a watch-guard for a watch, and is always seeing what time it is, and so there ain't nothing more to write about.

(Twain 1884: 360–2)

INTRODUCTION

The previous chapter established a common categorization of computer programs and written language in terms of the semiotic distinction of signifier, sign and signified. Although highly abstract, such an analysis is valuable in itself. It can now also be made more specific. An analogy, although not identity, of programs with pre-existing sign systems, with forms of writing, can be suggested. In order to substantiate this analogy, attention must be directed to the study of writing and the complex relation between writing and speech.

The discussion of writing, and its relation to speech, will itself be influenced by semiotics. Distinctions between types of sign, for instance between graphic and phonic signs, are derived from distinctions developed in, or influenced by, semiotics. The resistance to final definitions re-emerges as a difficulty in establishing exclusive distinctions between types of sign and then in assigning signs to these categories. Both speech and writing can be regarded as products of the semiotic faculty for producing signs. The very notion of a unified faculty for constructing socially shared systems of signs implies that differences between types of sign are unlikely to be absolute and that they may be complexly combined in human communication.

A semiotic approach to the differentiation of written from spoken language requires a methodological distinction between what are termed 'diachronic' and 'synchronic' perspectives. Diachrony refers to the consideration of a language, or other sign system, over time. For instance, tracing the etymology of words is a diachronic study. Synchrony refers to the consideration of a sign system at what is regarded as a single point in time. Synchronic linguistics is 'concerned with logical and psychological connexions between coexisting items constituting a system, as perceived by the same collective consciousness' (Saussure 1916: 98). Tracing the gradations of meaning and use which differentiate coexisting words in a language is a synchronic study. Discussions concede that it is difficult to maintain an absolute distinction between diachrony and synchrony. For instance, the etymology of a word need not determine its current synchronic meaning, but its history is liable to influence its current application. Synchrony is also acknowledged to be a highly useful construct, not a real existent. A synchronic state of a spoken language would be a period of relative stasis, of minimal change over a given period of time (Saussure 1916: 100). While acknowledging the difficulties of obtaining substantive distinctions between diachronic and synchronic features of sign systems, discussions tend to insist that clarity can only be obtained by enforcing a methodological distinction between synchronic and diachronic considerations.

The value of this methodological distinction for a consideration of the relations between written and spoken language, particularly for contrasting different synchronic states, can be exemplified. Most significantly, those synchronic states in which oral and written forms of a language coexist are not comparable with those in which oral discourse does not have an established correlate in writing. For instance, the ease with which a modern Western literate moves between written and spoken forms is not comparable with the social transition from primary orality to literacy, in the sense of communication by written language, in Ancient Greece. Pre-literacy, in this sense, is not to be confused with modern illiteracy. Similarly, the readiness with which modern literates can give oral correlates to forms of writing not intended as communicative substitutes for speech, such as ciphers for telegraphic transmission (Warner 1993) or computer

programming languages, contrasts with the mixture of appre-
hension and astonishment conveyed by the Cherokee reference to
the white man's 'talking leaves' (Harris 1986: 13). At an extreme,
it is possible to insist on distinguishing a multitude of synchronic
states, to demand that links between speech and writing need to
be separately established for each script, each language, each
period and each society (Morpurgo Davies 1986: 52). Yet,
although such subtle discrimination can be valuable in certain
contexts, and is a reminder of the complexity of the issues, it
could obscure a critical dimension which serves to distinguish a
series of synchronic states from another series of synchronic
states: the dimension of whether there was the possibility of
transcribing oral discourse to writing and whether a form of
writing closely associated with speech existed. Let us, then,
endorse the methodological distinction between diachrony and
synchrony, but also take the privilege of developing useful synchronic constructs from a multitude of potentially distinguishable synchronic states.

Such endorsement does not necessarily demand adoption of
the specialized semiotic vocabulary. Distinctions can be grasped
without resort to technical terms. For instance, Bishop John
Wilkins' comment that, although writing was historically subsequent to speech, 'yet in order of nature there is no priority
between these' (Wilkins 1668: 385) reveals a distinction analogous
to that of diachrony from synchrony. With regard to diachrony
and synchrony, ordinary discourse terms, such as historical and
contemporary, can convey necessary distinctions and also related
meanings: for instance, by referring to current Western practice,
other synchronic states can be implicitly excluded. In contrast,
the distinction of signifier, sign and signified gave a degree of
incisiveness, clarity and relative freedom from ambiguity difficult to obtain from ordinary discourse vocabulary. The methodological distinction between diachrony and synchrony is, then,
endorsed, but the specialized semiotic vocabulary will only be
employed where it conveys or reinforces distinctions difficult to
obtain from ordinary discourse terms.

Let us, then, first review the treatment of spoken and written
language in classic discussions of language; secondly, examine
possible distinctions between speech and writing, carefully distinguishing broadly contemporary contrasts from historical
differences; and, thirdly, develop a specialized vocabulary which

encourages not only a contrast of written with spoken language, but also distinctions between writing that draws on models in oral discourse and writing that is less strongly connected with speech. Programming can then be recognized as a form of writing not apparently intended to serve as a communicative substitute for speech.

HISTORICAL REVIEW

Discussions of language, both beyond and within linguistics, have tended to regard written language in alphabetic scripts as a secondary, derivative system of signs whose only function is to represent speech. The classic locus for this is the Aristotelian dictum: 'Spoken sounds are symbols of affections in the soul, and written marks symbols of spoken sounds' (Aristotle 323 BCb: 43). The substance of the dictum has been frequently reiterated in subsequent discussions of language: for example, in the seventeenth century Bishop John Wilkins characterized alphabetic writing as 'the picture or image of speech' (Wilkins 1668: 355).

Influential twentieth-century linguistic texts have adopted a similar position to their precursors, in this respect. For Saussure in the *Course in General Linguistics*, a language was a 'repository of sound patterns', linked to meanings, in which each element was synchronically interdependent. A change of item, for instance a shift in the relation between a sound-pattern and a meaning, would have repercussions throughout the entire system. Everything was internal to the system of a language whose change would alter the system in any respect. Writing was not internal to this system but gave 'tangible form' to speech (Saussure 1916: 15, 23–31, 113). Edward Sapir, in *Language: An Introduction to the Study of Speech*, regarded written language as a point-to-point equivalent to its spoken counterpart and echoed Aristotle: 'written forms are secondary symbols of the spoken ones – symbols of symbols' (Sapir 1921: 20). Exceptions to these assertions, and partial recognition of writing as an autonomous system of signs, can be found both in the texts cited and in other discussions of language, but the idea of written language as a secondary representation of speech has been dominant in classic discussions of language.

Although the dominant position within twentieth-century linguistics has been to regard written language as a secondary, derivative representation of speech, some forms of writing, particularly alphabetic scripts, have been implicitly or explicitly treated as if they captured the essential features of utterance. For Saussure, the alphabet could give fixed visual form to *la langue*, the spoken language which is held in common by a speech community, and does not represent *la parole*, utterances by individuals which can show variations from *la langue*. Discrepancies in correlation between spoken forms of *la langue* and written alphabetic sequences are ascribed to external causes, for instance to the tendency for writing to remain fixed while the spoken language evolves, not to any defect in the principle of representation (Saussure 1916: 15, 27–31; Harris 1987b: 40–5).

Chomsky's *Syntactic Structures* is little, if at all, indebted to Saussure but is of comparable influence. Chomsky tends implicitly to regard spoken and written forms of a language as equivalents to each other, with little explicit attention to mutual distinctions. The only difference noticed in the preliminary definition of a language ('a set [finite or infinite] of sentences, each finite in length and constructed out of a finite set of elements') is between construction out of phonemes and construction out of the letters of the alphabet of a language (Chomsky 1957: 13). However, the consistent, and uncritical, invoking of word and sentence boundaries in *Syntactic Structures* finds an equivalent only in some forms of written language, and not in oral discourse or all forms of written language. Neither the word nor the sentence has been satisfactorily isolated as a feature of utterance alone (Harris 1980).

The claim of some influential linguistic texts to be concerned primarily with spoken language then appears increasingly nominal. Alphabetic written language has tended to be taken as representing some of the essential features of utterance. It has deeply influenced linguistics, to the extent of providing the only historically existing equivalents to fundamental units sought or distinguished in spoken language (Harris 1980). Recognition of the extent of the influence of alphabetic written language on linguistics has been a recent, still incomplete and not necessarily widely accepted development (Harris 1980; Crystal 1985; 1987).

The concept of written language as a representation of speech has also tended to be accepted in wider discourse. For instance, the eleventh edition of the *Encyclopaedia Britannica*, published 1910–11, defined writing as 'the use of letters or other conventional characters for the recording by visible means of significant sounds' (*Encyclopaedia Britannica* 1911b: 852). The fifteenth edition, published in 1985, gave a slightly more expansive definition of writing as 'a system of human intercommunication by means of visible marks used conventionally' (*Encyclopaedia Britannica* 1985: 982). Within this broad definition two chronological stages were distinguished: pictures which did not have to correspond to elements in utterance; and phonography, or visual substitutes for elements of the oral language. Phonography included 'full writing', identified with alphabetic scripts. The term 'full writing' reveals a value judgement which prefers alphabetic writing to other scripts. Other forms of writing are taken to be stages in a progress towards an alphabetic ideal (*Encyclopaedia Britannica* 1985). The development of the concept of writing (from the earlier edition of the *Britannica*), does not therefore extend to granting equal value to non-alphabetic scripts.

The idea within linguistics of alphabetic writing as a representation of speech, and its acceptance in wider discourse, is matched by, and interlinked with, Western methods of inculcation into literacy. Thomas Sheridan, in a departure from the Aristotelian position, noted the influence of early education:

> We have in use two different kinds of language, which have no sort of affinity between them, but what custom has established; and which are communicated thro' different organs: the one, thro' the eye, by means of written characters; the other, thro' the ear, by means of articulate sounds and tones. But these two kinds of language are so early in life associated, that it is difficult ever after to separate them; or not to suppose that there is some kind of natural connection between them. And yet it is a matter of importance, always to bear in mind, that there is no sort of affinity between them, but what arises from an habitual association of ideas.
>
> (Quoted in Chapman 1984: 11)

Children are still commonly taught to take written signs as representations of spoken sounds. A convincing explanation for this practice has been given. Acquisition of skills in reading and writing is both a difficult and a prolonged process, essential to full participation in a literate society, and the acquisition of such skills may be eased by simplifying the relation between spoken and written forms of a language (Harris 1986: 89–90).

A representative relation between speech and written language is also easier to sustain, and to inculcate, in largely monoglot societies with a single alphabetic script, partially realized in the nation state of the developed West. A multilingual education is still possible within such societies and there is a detectable tendency for linguists to have a linguistically mixed upbringing. Saussure, for instance, was Swiss and, by the age of fifteen, had learned French, German, English, Latin and Greek (Culler 1976: 13). More recently, Chomsky came from an American Jewish background and his father was a Hebrew scholar (Lyons 1970: 117). An enforced early acquaintance with other languages and scripts may encourage a curiosity about language, even if this is not necessarily subsequently focused on the relation between spoken and written language. Yet educational emphasis on the close association of written and spoken language tends to ensure that modern Western literacy involves the integration in consciousness of speech and writing. Distinguishing spoken from written language then involves a struggle with received consciousness (Harris 1986).

WRITING AND SPEECH

The integration in consciousness of speech and writing may have been partially disturbed by changes in the relative communicative possibilities of spoken and written language since the mid-nineteenth century. Recorded or transmitted speech has partly usurped functions previously largely reserved to writing. Written language once had communicative possibilities denied to speech – the transmission of messages to receivers distant in space and time without immediate reliance on the memory of a human intermediary. The late nineteenth century inventions of the telephone (1876) and phonograph (1857–1877) enabled speech to be used for distant geographic and temporal communication. In turn, these audio media have been supplemented by audio-visual media, such as film and television, which can combine utterance and image for distant communication. The displacement of written language by recorded or transmitted speech for distant communication is sometimes described as secondary orality in contradistinction from the primary orality of societies without written language (Ong 1982). It has been accompanied by a re-examination of the relation of written to spoken language.

This has been facilitated by a practical consequence of audio-visual technologies. Before speech could be recorded, it could only be examined through memory or transcription and, if transcription was not intended for linguistic study, it might be altered to conform to expectations for written language: *Hansard* (the official report of the proceedings of the British Parliament), for instance, is discreetly edited to remove repetition and redundancies (Ollé 1973). 'Realistic' speech in novels can also be persuasively regarded as a convention adapted to fictional contexts and intentions (Page 1973; Chapman 1984). With the development of the tape-recorder in the 1940s, a phonetician was no longer condemned to wearing out sections of phonograph recordings (Crystal 1985: 59). Utterances can now be easily recorded and inspected and, with audio-visual technology, some gestural and situational supports to oral communication can also be recorded, rather than simply noted. Contrasts discovered can now be discussed, first from a synchronic and then from a diachronic perspective.

Contemporary contrasts

Extensive structural differences have been detected by comparison of written texts with accurately transcribed or recorded utterances. Differences between spoken and written language in acceptable word sequences and syntax have been discovered to be greatest when informal conversation is compared with written prose. However, even in formal settings, such as a lecture, the structure of spoken language has been found to bear little correspondence to writing. Pauses in speech do not correspond to word or sentence boundaries marked in writing. Word-order, when words have been identified in speech, is markedly different. Differences are still poorly documented, but are expected to continue to exceed early expectations (Crystal 1985: 21–3, 56–60; 1987: 178–9). Yet, at the same time, some discussions concede that structural variation among samples of utterances and of written language isolated for study can be as extensive as variation between spoken and written language (Biber 1988: 44).

There are also lexical differences between written and spoken languages, once words have been identified in utterance. Languages with written forms have much more extensive vocabularies than purely oral languages (Ong 1982: 8). Where written and spoken forms of a language coexist, the written form may contain items rarely pronounced: for instance, polysyllabic names for chemical compounds or some arcane legal terms are rarely spoken in contemporary English. Conversely, some spoken forms are rarely written and may not have a settled orthography: for example, 'whatdoyoucallit' (Crystal 1985: 179). Again, lexical contrasts within spoken and written language can be as great as differences between the two modes (Biber 1988: 24).

Lexical items distinguished from one another by their orthography are not necessarily differentiated in pronunciation. Diachronic influences, which may first aggravate and then reduce some contrasts, are detectable here. The orthography of vernacular documents became increasingly standardized after the development of printing (Gaur 1984: 205; Febvre and Martin 1976: 324–32) while spoken forms retained dialectal and personal peculiarities. Dialectal differences may then be diminished by the influence of the circulation of standardized vernacular texts. Samuel Johnson observed that 'the various dialects of the same country . . . will always be observed to grow fewer, and less different, as books are multiplied' (Johnson 1755b: 5). Spoken language may then be brought into a closer correspondence with a written form. Items with highly similar pronunciations may still be mutually distinguished by standardized orthography: for instance, 'rough' and 'ruff'. Pronunciation can differentiate items with identical spellings: English 'bow' as obeisance is distinguished in received pronunciation from 'bow' in 'bow window'. Significant distinctions can, then, be made by orthography which are not made by pronunciation; and by speech which are not necessarily reflected in written language.

The grounds for taking writing as a derivative representation of speech are weakened, but not entirely eroded, by the recognition of structural and lexical contrasts. Writing could still be regarded as an imperfect representation of speech. Such a defensive strategy for sustaining a representational relation has been weakened by a broadly concurrent perception that written language has expressive features without simple phonetic correlates in speech. There are no capital letters in utterance, although both spoken intonation and written capitalization, or its indication, can be used to convey emphasis:

> 'At such times as when your sister is on the Ram-page, Pip,' Joe sank his voice to a whisper and glanced at the door, 'candour compels fur to admit that she is a Buster.'

Joe pronounced this word as if it began with at least twelve capital Bs.

(Dickens 1861: 48)

Nor does speech have paragraphs, full stops, colons, commas or a direct equivalent to typographic spacing or different founts.

Some written genres, in particular graphic information systems, such as lists, catalogues and indexes, use punctuation marks, spatial organization and, often, different founts or weights of type to convey significant distinctions between entries or between elements of an entry (Reynolds 1979). Distinctions made between elements of a bibliographic entry can be rendered into speech or continuous prose, but only at greater length and with a possible reduction in clarity. Features of written language not present in utterance can then be used for expressive purposes difficult to achieve from utterance.

A conclusion on broadly contemporary contrasts between written and spoken language must be tempered by the inconclusive state of studies on this topic. Studies are incomplete, still developing and have not necessarily been methodologically compatible (Biber 1988: 49–51). Yet they do suggest that while inter-semiotic contrasts between speech and writing can be established with regard to such empirically detectable features as structure and vocabulary, intra-semiotic variation in these respects is as great. A subtle position can be developed which acknowledges inter- and intra-semiotic variations and the interconnections between spoken and written language. Rather than insisting on discovering absolute differences between speech and writing, or on writing as an independent communicative code, spoken and written language can productively be regarded as two, undeniably contrasting, ways of giving form to language: language is expressed through either writing or speech (Uldall 1944; Morpurgo Davies 1986: 52). Such a position does justice to the possibility of reading from writing to speech and transcribing speech to writing, and to the associated integration in modern Western literate consciousness of speech and writing. Let us, then, adopt this insistence on spoken and written language as different forms of a language as a position which will encompass a number of distinguishable synchronic states in which written and spoken forms of a language coexist, but which requires careful adaptation to specific historical conditions (a comparable position has been suggested for spoken and written Latin in Carolingian Europe [McKitterick 1989: 21]), and move to a consideration of a diachronic perspective on speech and writing.

Historical contrasts

Diachronic and synchronic considerations need to be mutually distinguished. The position endorsed for those synchronic states in which written and spoken forms of a language coexist is not necessarily relevant to other synchronic states without the possibilities of reading and transcription. Studies of the development of writing have not necessarily distinguished diachronic from synchronic perspectives and have tended to project the modern integration in consciousness of speech and of writing on to earlier scripts. For instance, they have been distorted by what is regarded as an alphabetic teleology, as if earlier scripts were striving to become the alphabet and were, as yet, imperfect representations of speech (Harris 1986). Historical studies of the relation between speech and writing have been accused of discrepancies between the limitations of discovered evidence and the elaborate reconstructions of the meaning and pronunciation of texts. For example, Mark Twain parodied nineteenth-century scholarly efforts at reading the geological record and deciphering ancient scripts, in an animal fable. Its conclusion remains sympathetic:

> There were vulgar, ignorant carpers, of course, as there always are and always will be; and naturally one of these was the obscene Tumble-Bug. He said that all he had learned by his travels was that science only needed a spoonful of supposition to build a mountain of demonstrated fact out of: and that for the future he meant to be content with the knowledge that nature had made free to all creatures and not go prying into the august secrets of the Deity.
>
> (Twain 1875: 121)

With these reservations in mind – that modern Western notions of literacy should not be projected on to other synchronic states and that speculation must be restrained by evidence – a historical perspective on the relation between speech and writing can be indicated.

Expressive features of written language such as word and sentence boundaries emerge as historically developed conventions. An early and widely used form of phonographic writing was the boustrophedon, 'the way an ox-drawn plough moves', a continuous thread in which neither word nor sentence boundaries were necessarily marked (Gaur 1984: 53–6). The convention of dividing written words from each other was not well established in Europe until the later medieval period (Harris 1980: 12). Phonographic and alphabetic writing have then had different conventions and expressive possibilities at different periods. If alphabetic written language is to be regarded as a simple representation of speech, then either the principles of representation, or the structure of speech itself, must have changed over time. The view of writing as merely a derivative system of signs becomes increasingly difficult to sustain.

Alphabetic writing is most persuasively regarded as a development from other graphic means of communication and information (Harris 1986). The phylogenetic priority of speech to writing has even been questioned. Bertrand Russell, in 1927, noted that speech had assumed functions once reserved for written language, of transmission of messages over space and time, and then speculated:

> I doubt whether it is even known whether writing or speech is the older form of language. The pictures made in caves by the Cro-Magnon men may have been intended to convey a meaning and may have been a form of writing. . . . it is not known to what extent pictures had been used in prehistoric times as a means of giving information or commands.
>
> (Russell 1927: 47)

Subsequent research seems to have lent some support to Russell's speculation on the early existence of graphic information systems (McArthur 1986: 18–20): for instance, it has been argued that artefacts surviving from the European Ice Age hunters of 30,000 BC bear a notation for recording the lunar cycle (Marschak 1972).

Historical evidence suggests that systems of reckoning came before the development of writing. For instance, the development of cuneiform script in Mesopotamia was preceded by the use of tokens, in the form of separate marked pieces of baked clay, apparently used to record transactions in grain, cattle, textiles and other necessities (Schmandt-Besserat 1978). Lists of objects, often compiled for administrative purposes such as taxation, and whose relation to utterance remains uncertain, have been characterized as the most archaic and pervasive of all genres (Goody 1977: 74–111). Other forms of graphic communication and writing existed before the development of alphabetic scripts, with variants of them in continuing use in societies with such scripts, and they need not be regarded as merely stages in a progress towards an alphabetic ideal.

Narratives about, and observations of, societies regarded as primarily oral testify to their ingenuity in devising non-oral forms of communication. Even the binary coding associated with computers has been anticipated. It seems to have been long understood that a binary contrast is sufficient for conveying information. Many codes, not necessarily subject to numerical interpretation, have been binary (Cherry 1957: 35). Two examples of binary codes, the one aural and the other graphic, will help illustrate this.

The Congo talking drum is reported to have used a binary contrast for the transmission of messages over space: 'The Dualla are in possession of an interesting code, in accordance with which messages can be sent and even conversations maintained by means of drums, or rather gongs, giving two notes' (*Encyclopaedia Britannica* 1910). From other accounts it appears that African drums were used for two types of communication: for direct transmission of language by tones which are taken as representing utterances in highly tonal languages; and for codes where pre-arranged signals represent a given message (Finnegan 1970: 481–99). Drum-signalling has been used in many cultures, from New Guinea to the old Mexicans, although accounts do not give a date of origin (Crawley 1931: 244–53).

In Plutarch's *Life of Theseus*, Theseus set out from Athens to slay the minotaur and to prevent further payment of tribute to Crete. A binary code linked to a message was arranged.

> Aegeus [Theseus' father] gave the pilot a second sail, a white one, and ordered him on the return voyage to hoist the white canvas if Theseus were safe, but otherwise to sail with the black as a sign of mourning.
>
> The story goes that as they approached the shore of Attica Theseus was so overcome by joy that he forgot, and so, too did his pilot, to hoist the sail which was to signal their safe return to Aegeus and he in despair threw himself down from the cliff and was killed.
>
> (Plutarch 100: 27–8)

A similar motif recurs in the later Tristan legend, although there, in one version at least, the signal is subject to deliberate mis-reporting, rather than accidental confusion.

> 'Caerdin, I [Tristan] do not know what I should ask you more urgently than what I now request: act as best you can and greet Brengvein warmly for me. Describe my malady to her, saying that unless God attend to it I shall die. . . . Take my fine ship and carry two yards on board, one with a white sail, the other with a black. If you can prevail upon Ysolt to come and heal my wound, use a white sail when returning. But if you do not bring Ysolt, then use the black!' . . .
>
> They have hoisted the white sail and are making good speed, when Caerdin espies the coast of Brittany. At this they are gay and light-hearted, they raise the sail right up so that can be seen what sail it is, the white or the black. Caerdin wished to show its colour from afar . . .
>
> While Tristan endures such affliction, his wife Ysolt comes and stands before him. Meditating great guile she says: 'Caerdin is coming, my love! I have seen his ship on the sea. I saw it making hardly any headway but nevertheless I could see it well enough to know that it is his. God grant it brings news that will comfort you at heart!'
>
> Tristan starts up at this news. 'Do you know for sure that it his ship, my darling?' he asks. 'Tell me now, what sort of sail is it?'
>
> 'I know it for a fact! answered Ysolt. 'Let me tell you, the sail is all black! They have hoisted it and raised it up high because they have no wind!'
>
> At this Tristan feels such pain that he has never had greater nor ever will, and he turns his face to the wall.
>
> (Von Strassburg 1215: 344–52)

Some aspects of these episodes deserve comment. Theseus is usually dated to the generation before the Trojan War. At that period, Athens did not have written language although Mycenean Crete had developed Linear B (Vico 1744; Gaur 1984: 69–70). In contrast, in the Tristan legend the episode occurs in the context of a society literate in the sense that some actors in the narrative also communicate by written language. Myths such as those of Theseus or Tristan themselves have an informative func-tion in primarily or strongly oral societies (Herodotus 430 BC; Vico 1744; Havelock 1982: 136). In this instance, the communities in which the myths were sustained had access to a sophisticated, if potentially unreliable, signalling system.

The motif is particularly interesting in its earlier context in the legend of Theseus, occurring prior to the adoption of written language by those involved in the construction, transmission and reception of the message. It can be analysed in terms of an influential model for communication partly derived from *The Mathematical Theory of Communication* (Shannon and Weaver 1949). The model involves a transmitter passing a message over a transmission channel to a receiver. Redundancy in the message can be valuable as it allows the original message to be reconstructed if it is corrupted by noise in the communication channel. On this model, the failure in communication from Theseus to Aegeus could be attributed to the vulnerability of signals without redundancy to corruption from noise in the communication channel. Evidence suggests that it is possible intuitively to grasp the value of redundancy in communication without acquaintance with the formal model of communication developed in *The Mathematical Theory of Communication* (Cherry 1957). The episode does raise the intriguing possibility that the original developers of those graphic communication systems we can now regard as alphabetic written language deliberately incorporated redundancy to preserve the meaning of messages transmitted over space. The most sophisticated reconstruction of the intentions of the devisers of alphabetic writing gives an account analogous to the conditions for economic and accurate transmission of messages established in *The Mathematical Theory of Communication*. However, there is no direct citation and the account does not distinguish between the preservation of information over time and the transmission of messages over space as well as time (Harris 1986). The issue cannot be fully explored in this context, but such an interpretation of the intentions of the devisers of alphabetic writing, as being primarily concerned with the transmission of messages over space, would accord with Vico's view of alphabetic writing as intended for epistolary communication (Vico 1744: 138–53).

A valuable conclusion can be obtained from these diachronic indications of contrasts between speech and writing. Once freed from the retrospective projection of a Western literate consciousness formed by the experience of reading and transcription, the possibility of forms of writing radically independent of utterance emerges. Some forms of writing may never have been read to speech by their producers or immediately intended receivers, and their oral discourse may not have been given graphic correlates. These hints have been partially obscured by the alphabetical teleology which has characterized some historical studies of writing.

A feature of writing which emerges as relatively constant from both synchronic and diachronic considerations is its graphic nature. It has no distinctive visual characteristics by which it can consistently be distinguished from other graphic forms, such as decoration (Harris 1986: 16). Unknown scripts can be confused with designs: for instance, it was unclear in the early stages of excavation in Mesopotamia whether the wedge-shaped cuneiform signs were writing or decoration (Gaur 1984: 140). Alphabetic written language can still be regarded as a form of graphic signification.

The assertion that writing is a form of graphic signification needs careful delimitation. It does not imply that writing cannot be made auditorily intelligible by human reading to oral discourse or mechanical transformation to distinguishable sounds. Nor does the assertion that writing is part of the graphic imply that speech is not, in some circumstances, also graphic. An oral discourse may have visually interpretable elements, such as speakers' relative positions and posture, which can be significant to its interpretation. Some more sophisticated distinctions between types of graphic sign are needed to develop the insight into the nature of writing and to elucidate its relation to speech.

METALANGUAGE

A metalanguage, or, in the sense intended here, a specialized vocabulary for discussing another sign-system, can either yield, or disguise, significant distinctions. The aim of this section is to develop a metalanguage, based on the insight that alphabetic written language can be regarded as a form of graphic signification, and then to exemplify the powerful and subtle distinctions it can yield, continuing to differentiate diachronic from synchronic considerations.

Metalinguistic distinctions for classifying and discussing forms of writing have been influenced by the privileged status accorded to the alphabet. Recognition of the affinities of alphabetic writing with other forms of writing and graphic signification has emerged, with some exceptions, as a recent development. The superiority of the alphabet, and its status as a teleological ideal, tended to be accepted in Western discussions of the development of writing (Derrida 1976: 26; Harris 1986). A complex and distorted metalanguage for classifying scripts, with distinctions based on implicit or explicit contrasts with the alphabet, has resulted. Pictographic, ideographic, logographic, syllabic and alphabetic signs have typically been distinguished (Harris 1986; Morpurgo Davies 1986). Some trace of the complexity of such classifications could be discerned in the treatment of writing in the later edition of the *Encyclopaedia Britannica* where alphabetic or 'full writing' had to be awkwardly distinguished from other phonographic scripts and from preceding pictorial forms (*Encyclopaedia Britannica* 1985).

A simpler and more incisive metalanguage can be obtained by concentrating on differentiations between forms of graphic signification. Within the graphic, the pictorial and scriptorial can be distinguished from each other. A scriptorial sign is given meaning from its place in an established system of signs, whereas a pictorial sign need not, although it may, obtain its meaning in this way. For instance, the familiar sequence of traffic lights could be regarded as a scriptorial system in which the meaning of different synchronic states depends upon their mutual difference. No definition of the pictorial is attempted beyond an appeal to an ostensive exemplification, such as a photographic portrait of a person. A pictorial sign can be iconic in the sense of there being a visual similarity between signifier and signified, but this need not be the case, and the degree of iconicity is open to question. A diagram may help to clarify the relation between the graphic, the pictorial and the scriptorial:

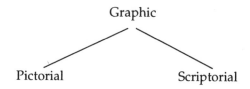

The contrast between the scriptorial and the pictorial helps to establish the sense of each opposed term.

Writing would be included in the scriptorial. Writing itself can be subdivided, for analytical purposes, into writing which draws on models in oral discourse and writing which does not. Again, a diagram may make this classification clearer:

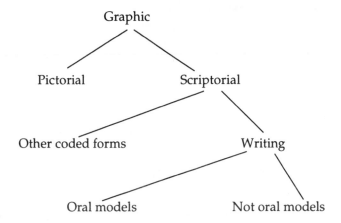

The term 'written language' will be, and has been, reserved for writing which does draw on models in oral discourse, such as some, although not all, uses of alphabetic scripts. Such differentiations – between the pictorial and the scriptorial, and between writing which draws on oral models and writing which does not – are analytical, not necessarily substantive, distinctions.

The boundaries between the pictorial and scriptorial are indefinite and subject to alteration. Changes in technologies for painting, drawing and writing can influence the distinction of the scriptorial from the pictorial. Russell, for instance, in questioning the diachronic priority of speech to writing implied that Cro-Magnon man may not have had an equivalent to this boundary (Russell 1927: 47). Some currently used signs and media combine or mix the pictorial and scriptorial. For example, letters of the alphabet may be adapted in trademarks to form a picture comparable to the object or idea denoted by the alphabetic sequence adapted: the abbreviation BSI, for the British Standards Institution, is adapted to form a kitemark intended as a sign of quality.

Other graphic signs, particularly those intended to convey information translingually, can legitimately be interpreted either pictorially, as an image for an object, or scriptorially, within a set of established conventions for similar signs. For example, a road-sign showing a silhouette of a cow on a white background within a red border can be interpreted pictorially, and, in this instance, iconically, as an image of a cow, or read as a warning of the possible presence of cattle. Context and purpose of inter-pretation, whether in an art gallery or from a car, may be crucial to determining whether a pictorial or scriptorial interpretation is dominant for such signs. Mixing, rather than combining, scrip-torial and pictorial signs may be more common contemporary Western practice. For instance, the bare form of some modern printed books, where a functional clarity is expected by authors (McKenzie 1986: 24) and in which a clear distinction tends to be implied between writing and illustration, both exemplifies and may tend to encourage a harsh distinction of the pictorial from the scriptorial.

Distinctions can be made within the scriptorial, for instance, to differentiate forms and functions of writing. Different types of writing could be distinguished by their graphic form, by relation to other sign-systems, by communicative function or by social centrality. The graphic form of the Roman alphabet could be used to distinguish it from other scripts, such as Cyrillic or Hebrew. The extent to which a form of writing draws on models in a distinguishable sign-system, such as oral discourse, could be used to differentiate it from other forms of writing. Phonographic writing would then be isolated by its connection with speech. Communicative functions intended for forms of writing can be usefully distinguished along dimensions of time and space, and of public and private. The communicative intentions of pub-lished documents, for transmission over space and time to largely unknown readers, are different from those of monumental inscriptions or signs for street names, intended primarily for preservation over time and from private correspondence directed to a known addressee. The social centrality of alphabetic written language in developed Western societies can be used to distin-guish it from other contemporary forms of writing such as musical or choreographic notation.

Differentiations between forms of writing are not mutually independent or exclusive. A script identified by its graphic form may complexly traverse other distinctions: the Roman alpha-bet, for instance, may be used for ciphers without a direct oral model, for transmission over space and time, and for preservation primarily over time. The most familiar principle chosen, implicitly or explicitly, for classification has been by relation to another sign-system – to spoken language. The alphabetic scripts which tend to be isolated by this principle have been used, although not exclusively, for both distant spatial and temporal communication.

Some of the possible distinctions between forms of writing are particularly significant to the categorization of computer programming in relation to pre-existing forms of writing and to a consideration of the historical context of the *Phaedrus*, the dialogue which gives Plato's objections to written language and which will be discussed in the next chapter. The distinction between forms of writing which draw on oral models and writing which does not is relevant to the classification of programming. The contrast between forms of writing which are used primarily for transmission over time and those which are used for transmission over space and time, and between public and private dissemination, is crucial to an understanding of Plato's accusation that written language does not have the capacity for dialectic response only obtainable from a human speaker. Distinctions made are intended for analytical purposes and not as final, mutually exclusive, categories. They require further development and exmplification.

The distinction between forms of writing which have no necessary connection with utterance and forms which draw on oral models for the purposes of graphic communication can be discovered in both historical and contemporary contrasts. A historical contrast is that between Egyptian hieroglyphics and syllabic or alphabetic written language. In one widely held interpretation, to which there are exceptions, Egyptian hieroglyphics are seen as coded marks standing directly for objects and having no necessary connection with utterance: 'hieroglyphic writing . . . pictures the facts it describes' (Wittgenstein 1922: 67). There is the possibility that hieroglyphics may have been radically silent in the sense that they were not associated with coexisting forms of oral discourse. Syllabic or alphabetic written language can be regarded as a development from pre-existing forms of writing but distinguished by the extent to which it draws on models in another sign-system – in spoken language – for the purposes of graphic communication (Harris 1986). A contemporary distinction between writing which draws on oral models and writing possibly independent of spoken language can be found in the contrast between alphabetic written language and mathematical notations, the object-language of a symbolic logic or computer programming languages. In contrast to possible historical antecedents, these non-oral forms of writing which coexist with written languages may be associated with speech by their producers and receivers. They can, under certain circumstances, be read to utterance, but have no direct connection with oral models and are not apparently intended as communicative substitutes for spoken language. There may be a loss of clarity when oral substitutes are supplied for the purposes of discussion. For instance, the logical expression for material implication, '$p \rightarrow q$', can be given the verbal correlate, 'If p then q', and is then more readily read to speech. Difficulties in interpretation have tended to follow from the confusion generated between the definition of '$p \rightarrow q$' in formal logic, as equivalent to '$\sim p \vee q$', and the meanings 'If p then q' can assume in wider discourse, where a necessary or causal connection between antecedent and consequent may be implied (Quine 1937: 84). The term 'writing' will continue to be used to cover all forms of writing, and 'written language' reserved for writing which has strong links with utterance.

The distinction between oral and non-oral forms of writing enables the influential Aristotelian doctrine that writing is a secondary system of signs, parasitic on speech, to be questioned in two respects. First, the doctrine is not easily applicable to non-oral forms of writing, particularly to those historical forms which may have been radically silent, and would have to be uncomfortably stretched to encompass contemporary non-oral forms. Secondly, Aristotle's assertion that writing is a secondary symbolism for speech has often been interpreted to imply a representative relation between speech and writing, although the precise nature of the representation is not necessarily specified (Harris 1986). The nature of the relation between speech and writing, for forms of writing strongly associated with oral discourse, needs to be clarified.

For such oral forms of writing, the relation of visual written forms to invisible spoken sounds is one of conventional correlation, not of representation based on similarity: there is no resemblance between the written word 'should' and its spoken form. There is, however, a set of conventions, with historically developed irregularities, which give instructions for the pronunciation of written sequences and for the writing of spoken sequences. Even if orthographic irregularities did not exist, the relationship of written to spoken forms would remain one of correlation, not of representation (Harris 1986).

The example of choreographic notation may make the distinction between correlation and representation easier to grasp, as the integration in consciousness of the written code and dance movements is less widely stressed in early education. Choreographic notations, of which there are different systems, are coded marks which can be correlated by known instructions to significant points in movement (Guest 1985). They are not a representation comparable to that given by a moving film or a videotape of a dance. Similarly, alphabetic written language is not a representation of speech comparable to that obtainable from audiovisual media.

Correlation from spoken to written forms, however consistent, is inevitably incomplete. An uttered linguistic sequence consists of numerous sounds: phonographic writing can only indicate certain significant features of such a sequence. Spoken language has intonational features typically not recorded, although sometimes indicated by added comments, in alphabetic writing. Correlation from spoken to written language also involves translating a sequence extended in time into one extended in space. Evidence also suggests that the degree of segmentation of utterances encouraged by correlation from alphabetic writing, into consonants and vowels, is more difficult to achieve than division into syllables. Syllable-sized segments have been regarded as more convincing as minimum units for the processes involved in speech production and perception; and syllabaries have been developed independently, whereas the alphabet was only invented once (Harris 1986: 120). There is then no resemblance as such between written language and speech: writing can only indicate particular features of a continuously varying utterance, extended over time not space, and alphabetic writing requires a highly contrived degree of segmentation of speech.

The distinction which can be made between forms of writing intended for transmission over time alone and over both space and time is applicable to both non-oral and oral forms of writing. It can also be discerned in historical and contemporary contrasts. Egyptian hieroglyphics, for instance, have been found predominantly, although not exclusively, as monumental inscriptions (Diringer 1968: 29–34; Gaur 1984: 35–6, 61–5, 140; Young

1823: 12–16, 55). Later, and contemporary, inscriptions, such as those found on gravestones, could be differentiated from documents. The interpretation of inscriptions can be crucially dependent on their spatial context: '*Si monumentum requiris, circumspice*' originally required the setting of St Paul's cathedral to obtain its meaning as a testimony to Sir Christopher Wren. The historical and contemporary cases differ significantly: historically, there is the possibility of forms of writing used predominantly or solely for the preservation of information over time; in contemporary practice, alphabetic written language can be used primarily for preservation over time, for transmission over space, and for both purposes. Earlier, it was suggested that the redundancy detectable in alphabetic written language was associated with the need to transmit messages across space with minimal ambiguity. The term 'inscription' will be used for writing intended for preservation over time and 'document' for forms of writing transmitted over space and time.

The scope given here to the terms inscription and document is subtly, although still significantly, different from the meanings the terms can obtain in relevant specialized and ordinary discourse. Epigraphy and palaeography are both studies concerned, in contrasting ways, with the recovery and transcription of written communication. Epigraphy focuses on writing on hard materials and tends to refer to its objects of study as inscriptions; palaeography is principally concerned with handwriting on soft materials (Diringer 1968: 2) and may refer to its objects of study as documents. In ordinary discourse, the terms can carry similar, although not necessarily deliberately delimited, senses both to the meanings assigned here and to the distinction between objects of study for epigraphy and palaeography: an inscription might be writing on hard material, which could also be spatially fixed; a document might be a portable artifact with writing on a soft medium.

The distinctions made here, between preservation over time and transmission over space and time, may, in some respects, be positively associated with both the specialized and ordinary discourse senses of inscription and document. For instance, artefacts regarded as inscriptions in the epigraphic sense of writing on hard material may also be intended for preservation over time in a fixed location; similarly, a handwritten letter, potentially subject to palaeographic analysis and transcription, may also be intended for transmission over space and time. Yet there can also be significant contrasts: for example, marks engraved on clay tablets could be regarded as inscriptions from an epigraphic perspective but may be intended for transmission over space; conversely, handwriting on wax tablets could be considered the province of palaeography, although little is known to have survived from the classical periods (Rouse and Rouse 1989), but might be primarily intended for private recollection over time rather than dissemination over space. The scope assigned here to the terms inscription and document is, then, more systematic and deliberate than their ordinary discourse uses, and, in contrast to the distinction by physical medium, reflected in the differentiation of epigraphy from palaeography, embodies dimensions of social significance, of preservation over time distinguished from communication over space and time.

Documents can be further distinguished into private and public forms, although this boundary is subject to historical change and to different interpretations. For instance, the scientific journal emerged from less public, although not fully private, scientific correspondence (Watson *et al.* 1973). In contemporary terms, it may be difficult to agree on a demarcation between private and public forms: at what point, for instance, does a report whose circulation is deliberately restricted became a public document? Committees convened to review United Kingdom copyright legislation, which requires legal deposit only for published documents, not for inscriptions or private correspondence, have found it difficult to define publication, although a criterion of transmission to a largely unknown audience distant in space and time has tended to be implicitly invoked (Report of the Copyright 1952: 25–6; Copyright and Designs 1977: 207). For instance, it has been considered that works issued solely for the use of members of research associations were not to be regarded as publications for the purposes of legal deposit. Availability to the general public was to be the determining principle (Report of the Copyright 1952: 25–6).

These distinctions, between writing related to oral models and writing independent of spoken language, between writing intended for preservation over time and transmission over space and time, and between public and private documents, are relevant to a common dimension: the possibility of direct interrogation of the producer of a statement and of immediate acquaintance with its social or spatial context. Writing which draws on oral models can be used as a substitute for the presence of a live speaker, possibly open to questioning. Assertions in written language tend to be protected from the immediate questioning often possible with unrecorded speech. If writing is transmitted over space as well as time, the opportunity for acquaintance with its original context is liable to be diminished. For published documents, as distinct from correspondence, the opportunity of immediate dialogue with the producer tends further to be reduced greatly. The opportunity for questioning the producer of a statement, and for immediate knowledge of its context, has been called openness to direct semantic ratification (Ong 1982: 47). It tends to be a highly consistent, although still not absolute, contemporary difference between written language and unrecorded speech (Biber 1988: 44).

A final, admittedly imprecise but still valuable, dimension for differentiating forms of writing and other systems of signs is their synchronic social significance. Alphabetic written language is evidently important to modern Western societies. In other circumstances, coded gestures may be socially significant: for example, the American Plains Indians used a gesture language for communication between tribes speaking mutually incomprehensible languages (*Encyclopaedia Britannica* 1985: 983). Similarly, for hearing-impaired members of contemporary Western societies, sign languages may be important. The mere existence of a sign-system does not guarantee its social significance. For instance, the development of copyright in the sense of intellectual property in the United Kingdom and the United States suggests that the social significance of computer programming to those political communities grew gradually, impinging first on the judiciary and then emerging in legislative deliberations in the late 1970s, some thirty years after the development of the stored program computer (Warner 1993).

In conclusion, the metalinguistic distinctions for writing and its relation to speech have been developed not as an artefact valuable in itself but in order to give systematic, but flexible, dimensions along which to consider elusive and historically variable contrasts between forms of writing and between writing and speech. The distinction of oral from non-oral forms of writing enabled the doctrine that writing is a representation of speech, traceable to Aristotle, to be questioned. Its applicability to non-oral forms of writing, particularly those existing before the development of written language, was suggested to be doubtful. For oral forms of writing, the notion of representation had to be replaced by correlation. Time and space dimensions were also differentiated and marked by the ordinary discourse terms 'inscription' and 'document', used in carefully delimited senses. Distinctions established between oral and non-oral forms of writing, between inscriptions and documents, and between public and private documents were all crucial to the dimension of semantic ratification – the extent to which the producer of a discourse can be asked to explain it. The final dimension established – that of social significance – alerts us to the current significance of alphabetic written language and computer programming.

CONCLUSION

A review and summary of the main themes of this chapter are appropriate here. Classic discussions of language tended to regard written language as a secondary system of signs, simply derivative from speech. Education into literacy still tends to involve integrating speech with writing. Differentiating the two involves a struggle with received consciousness. Linguistics has, to some extent, both inherited and sustained the integration of spoken and written language. Speech tends to be advanced as the nominal object of linguistic study. But, by treating written language in alphabetic scripts as if it captured the essential features of utterance, writing tends to become the actual, although often concealed, focus (Harris 1980). Equivalents to units of language distinguished in some forms of writing are then sought in speech. The concealed focus on written language, and the search for equivalents in speech to units distinguished in written language, have impeded recognition and documentation of differences. Registering of differences between written and spoken forms of a language is still severely incomplete. The technical developments – audio and audio-visual media – which have partly prompted, and have facilitated, a re-examination of the relation of written to spoken language remain in advance of conceptual changes. Recognition and documentation of differences are still sufficient to warrant an insistence on distinguishing written from spoken language.

Recent research, partly stimulated and aided by technical developments in audio and audio-visual media, has detected extensive lexical and structural contrasts between written and spoken language. Extensive differences can be detected between the synchronically coexisting written and spoken forms of a language. Acceptable word-order, and the construction of sequences, are different. There are lexical differences between spoken and written languages, in extent of vocabulary, with some written words rarely spoken and some spoken sequences rarely recorded. Distinctions between lexical items can be made in written language or in speech which are not necessarily registered in the other medium. Pauses in speech do not correspond to written boundaries, such as spaces between words or punctuation marks. Some genres of written language, particularly information systems such as lists, catalogues and indexes, use graphic elements to make distinctions that are more difficult to obtain with similar clarity in speech.

Such synchronic contrasts between written and spoken forms of a language seldom constitute absolute differences (Biber 1988: 24). Some can be highly consistent, such as the relative openness of unrecorded speech to questioning in contrast to the possibility of the distant reception of written language and its removal from immediate questioning. Other contrasts – for instance, the relative permanency of writing when compared to speech – have been weakened by the development of technologies for recording and transmitting utterances which have conferred the possibility of permanency on speech. A subtle position could be obtained. Rather than insisting on absolute contrast between spoken and written forms of a language, or on the autonomy of the written language as a system of signs, they could both be regarded as two contrasting ways of giving form to language.

Diachronic considerations indicated deeper levels of difference between writing and speech. The position suggested for those synchronic states in which written and spoken forms of a language coexist is not applicable to those states in which oral discourse does not have a written correlate. Alphabetic written language is most persuasively seen as a development from other graphic information systems. The phylogenetic priority of speech to writing has even been questioned. Systems of reckoning and forms of writing whose relation to utterance remains uncertain are known to have preceded the development of those graphic systems of signs we can now regard as written languages. Narratives about and from primarily oral societies testify to their ingenuity in devising forms of graphic signification and communication. Historical considerations, then, suggested that an association with utterance is not necessary for graphic signification to be regarded as writing.

A characteristic of writing which emerged as relatively constant from both historical and contemporary considerations was its graphic nature. A metalanguage was developed to reflect and refine this insight. Within the graphic, the pictorial was distinguished from the scriptorial, and writing was regarded as part of the scriptorial. Oral forms of writing were differentiated from non-oral forms of writing, carefully distinguishing historical from broadly contemporary cases. For forms of writing with established oral correlates, the received notion that writing is a representation of speech, however construed, had to be replaced by an idea of correlation. Other dimensions for classifying writing, such as preservation over time, transmission across space and time, public and private dissemination, and the degree of openness to semantic ratification, were developed. They could be applied to both oral and non-oral manifestations of writing. The aim of the metalanguage was not to develop rigid categories but to give a sophisticated framework for the analysis of elusive and historically variable contrasts between forms and communicative functions of writing and between writing and speech.

Recognition of synchronic contrasts between written and spoken language, and of the affinities of written language with other forms of writing such as choreographic and musical notation, and the diachronic filiation of written languages from other forms of graphic signification, including possibly non-oral forms of writing, can lead to a subtle position. Connections between written and spoken language, and the integration in modern Western literate consciousness of speech and of writing, can be acknowledged. One form of writing, exemplified by alphabetic written languages, draws on oral models, and can function as a communicative substitute for spoken language, but a connection to speech is not necessary for the recognition of writing. The position warrants some emphasis: it acknowledges a link between spoken and written language, does justice to their linguistic nature, and, simultaneously, does not make a relation to oral models an exclusive criterion for writing.

From this position, computer programming can be regarded as a form of writing, apparently never intended as a communicative substitute for speech. The close integration of writing and speech in literate consciousness ensures that programming languages can be given verbal and oral substitutes for the purposes of written and spoken discussion, although there may be a loss of clarity or exactness in the process. The design and construction of programming languages is also liable to have been affected, both unconsciously and deliberately, by models available in pre-existing forms of writing, such as written languages and logical and mathematical symbolisms, and by categories developed for the grammatical analysis of the written sentence. They seem to differ from these pre-existing analogues not so much in their graphic form or susceptibility to pronunciation as in their function of prescribing a set of logical operations for a computer. This assertion will be developed, and the nature of those logical operations, including the relation between a program and a computer, will be discussed in greater depth, in Chapter 4.

Each change in technologies for writing and for communication affects the boundaries given to the scriptorial. Subsequent to and then concurrent with the development of audio and audio-visual media, and with the writing of computer programs, has been a linked recognition of contrasts between written and spoken language and of the affinities of written language with forms of writing with no simple or necessary correlate in utterance. That a written expression in the form of a computer program can, as a working automaton, be given a graphic display, which may include pictorial elements, may further modify the boundary between the pictorial and the scriptorial. The interpretation of writing has already markedly changed in some linguistic discussions (Harris 1986) and in British and American copyright law (Warner 1993).

Changes in consciousness have tended to lag behind the technical developments which have partly motivated them. Written language has been only incompletely disentangled from speech. Secondary orality grew self-conscious long after the late nineteenth-century inventions, the telephone and phonograph, which first enabled speech partly to displace writing for distant communication. The received idea of written language as a representation of speech seems to have had a grip from which it was difficult, even partially, to escape until the communicative functions of spoken and written language were radically disturbed.

Chapter 3

Intelligence of documents

> The man with real knowledge of right and beauty and good . . .
> will not take a pen and write in water or sow his seed in the
> black fluid called ink.
>
> (Plato 400 BCb: 98–9)

INTRODUCTION

The perspective established here which links computers directly
with documents through writing and through the human faculty
for constructing socially shared systems of signs represents a
radical departure from an immediate analogy between the computer and the human brain or mind. From such a viewpoint, it
can be shown that claims for the literal intelligence of an appropriately programmed computer, in the tradition established by
the Turing test, have rested on a similar basis to claims for the
intelligence of a document. In this context, the term *literal*
intelligence is used in contradistinction from the appearance of
intelligence, without its substance. The term intelligence is intended
to cover both its substance and appearance, unless it is qualified
or the context clearly indicates otherwise. To recall a methodological qualification from the introduction: the concept of
intelligence will be elucidated to some extent – for instance, it will
be connected with the faculty for arranging signs – and different
aspects of intelligence distinguished, but no final definition
attempted.

In the Turing test, a computer was required to respond to
questions with depersonalized linguistic output sufficiently
sophisticated to deceive the questioner into believing that the
response could have come from a human subject. Similarly, a

publicly circulated document could be said to make depersonalized language available. Claims for the literal intelligence of computers and documents are subject to an identical objection – that such linguistic output is made available without a prior act of comprehension by the artefact. Such a position would be tenable on purely logical grounds, from the perspective established here, but it is also supported by historical evidence.

In order to substantiate this, a complaint that documents offer only the appearance of intelligence, without its substance, must be examined. This complaint, in Plato's *Phaedrus* (Plato 400 BCb), needs to be seen in its historical context – the supplementing of oral communication by written language in the Ancient Greek world (Goody and Watt 1963). The concern, then, is not with the disappointing results of attempts at simulation of human intelligence, but simply with showing that there are extensive similarities between claims for, and objections to, computer and documentary intelligence.

TRANSITIONS FROM PRIMARY ORALITY

A feature of secondary orality is the attention given to earlier transitions in methods for communicating and storing information. The transition from primary orality in Ancient Greece has been a strong, but not exclusive focus of attention (Goody and Watt 1963; Havelock 1982; Ong 1982; Harris 1986). It tends to be regarded as a particularly pure, and subsequently significant, case for a study of the cultural effects of a transition from primary orality. The introduction of alphabetic written language to Greece has been considered to be the prime historical example of a transition to a literate society, without the import of other cultural features (Goody and Watt 1963: 42). The *Phaedrus* has emerged as a crucial text, although not free from difficulties in interpretation (Harris 1989). The *Phaedrus* must be placed in the context of the progressive supplementing of direct oral communication by written language removed from its producer.

The idea that documents could have been attributed the appearance of intelligence may gain credibility from considering the depth of anxieties that can be associated with the introduction of writing, as revealed in narratives from and about primarily or strongly oral societies. A consideration of such narratives, and of the historical context of the *Phaedrus*, needs to be informed by the distinctions between forms of writing, and between writing and speech, developed in the previous chapter: between forms of writing which draw on oral models and writing which does not; between forms of writing which are used primarily for transmission over time and those which are used for transmission over space and time; and between public and private documents. To reiterate, distinctions made are intended for analytical purposes and not as final, mutually exclusive categories.

An incident indicative of the possible impact of writing on a primarily oral culture, which would probably have been familiar to Plato from the significance of Homer in Greek education (revealed in *The Republic* [Plato 375 BC]), occurs in *The Iliad*. Bellerophon was given a message which he could not interpret and which required the recipient to kill him. Bellerophon had been under the power of King Proetus. Queen Anteaia had falsely informed the king that Bellerophon had tried to rape her:

> Rage filled the king
> over her slander, but being scrupulous
> he shrank from killing him. So into Lycia
> he sent him, charged to bear a deadly cipher,
> magical marks Proetus engraved and hid
> in folded tablets. He commanded him
> to show these to his father-in-law,
> thinking in this way he should meet his end. . . .
> When he had read the deadly cipher, changing
> he gave his first command.
>
> (Homer 750 BCa: 102–4)

Bellerophon survived the series of trials imposed upon him.

The episode is commonly taken as the only allusion to writing in Homer (Harris 1986: 15), although there is an inconclusive, and probably unresolvable, scholarly debate as to the nature of the writing. Considerations based on chronologies established from historical evidence must be tempered by the recognition that the cultural portrait offered by Homer is best regarded as a conflation of accounts originating at different periods (Kirk 1985: 5). However, the relative lack of allusions to writing has been considered to reflect conditions in Greece after the obsolescence of Mycenaean Linear B and before the wide diffusion of alphabetic writing (Kirk 1985: 9). The marks inscribed by Proteus have been regarded as a memory of Linear B, of Hittite hieroglyphics or of Cypriot syllabary, rather than a reference to the new alphabetic script. More tentatively, and more satisfyingly, it is conceded that the allusion is vague and indirect and the marks could be any kind of message bearing signs. Clay or wood coated with wax have been suggested as the substrate for the inscription (Kirk 1990: 181). The categorization of the inscribed signs as writing would tend to imply a connection with utterance.

Aspects of the narrative itself can illuminate, although not resolve, the issue of whether the writing was strongly associated with utterance by its addresser or addressee. The message is not dictated to a scribe, if the possibility of transcribing utterance existed, but engraved directly on a substrate. The absence of a scribal class from the complex and highly organized household of Odysseus has been remarked (Kirk 1985: 9). Nor is the message read to utterance by its addressee; it is silently comprehended. Silent reading was unusual in the Ancient Greek and Roman world, even for solitary reading, for those subsequent forms of writing definitely known to be associated with utterance (Illich and Sanders 1988: 51). Augustine, for instance, regards silent solitary reading as sufficiently unusual to be worthy of report: 'When he [Ambrose] read, his eyes scanned the page and his heart explored the meaning, but his voice was silent and his tongue was still' (Augustine 398: 42). The practice of silent reading did not become widespread in Europe until printing from moveable type made it possible for documents to be reproduced with less labour than copying manuscripts involved (Goody and Watt 1963: 42; Febvre and Martin 1976). The writing is not, then, associated with utterance in the episode, by either its addresser or addressee, and may have been a radically silent, non-oral form. The narrative motif can recur with forms of writing with established oral correlates, for instance in Claudius' attempt to dispose of Hamlet (Harris 1986: 15).

The episode of Bellerophon has been regarded as reminiscent of the practice of killing the slave who brought bad news (Harris 1986: 16), recalled in Cleopatra's extravagant threat, 'Thou shalt be whipp'd with wire and stew'd in brine/Smarting in ling'ring pickle' (Shakespeare 1600: 1167), yet there is also a significant contrast. The practice of killing the messenger, traceable to primarily oral societies, could be regarded as indicative of the absence of a strong disassociation of the messenger from the message, of the abstraction 'language' from the existential context of oral communication. For instance, the primarily oral Gbeya were not concerned with speech as a semantic domain, did not have explicit notions of grammatical correctness, and regarded bad speech as what causes trouble between people (Samarin 1969). It is left to the strongly literate and logical Roman messenger subtly to distinguish the bearer from the content of communication: 'I that do bring the news made not the match' (Shakespeare 1600: 1167). The transmission of the message in the episode of Bellerophon can be placed in terms of the deliberately developed distinctions between preservation over time and transmission across space and time. The message is transmitted primarily over space and only secondarily over time. Although, from an epigraphic perspective, the writing could be regarded as an inscription, it is a document in terms of the metalanguage suggested. The personal inscription of the writing by King Proitos, and of lots by other central actors in the narrative, implies at least a degree of social diffusion of writing. Archaeological evidence does indicate that writing was not an esoteric art in early Greece (Morpugo Davies 1986: 58). However, the message carried by Bellerophon is in the nature of a deliberately private, and secret, communication rather than assisting the communal preservation of information over time.

The episode of Bellerophon tends to be considered in isolation from other forms of humanly constructed graphic signification, although analogues can be found in other episodes. In some instances, the medium for signification, and even the process of inscription, are similar to the signs regarded as writing, particularly if the substrate there is taken to be clay. For instance, there a number of incidents in *The Iliad* which involve the recognition of lots, by central actors of the narrative, as personal identifiers in the form of stones cast from a helmet (Homer 750 BCc: 139, 220, 570, 586). In one instance, the lots are inscribed as well as recognized:

> And each soldier scratched his mark on a stone
> and threw it into Atrides Agamemnon's helmet.
>
> (Homer 750 BCc: 220)

In this episode, participants are able to recognize their own lot and to distinguish it from other lots, but, apparently although not conclusively, able to link lots with other participants. Although there may be resemblances in medium to the signs regarded as writing, there are contrasts in function: the process of recognition is communal, rather than deliberately secret; and the lots are not transmitted over space. In some discussions, these episodes are ignored (Harris 1986), or, where they are noticed, sharply distinguished as signs, not letters (Kirk 1990: 258).

The appearance of a radical novelty which might attach to the writing in the episode of Bellerophon can be further diminished when the writing is placed in the context of other forms of graphic signification recounted by Homer. In addition to inscribed lots, there are other forms of deliberate graphic signification, not similar in media. For instance, Penelope's weaving and unweaving of her father's shroud can be interpreted as an image of the oral narrative of *The Odyssey* (Heubeck and Hoekstra 1989: 61, 80–2, 374–6), with its temporal discontinuities and recapitulations, particularly when the etymology of 'rhapsodize' from a root meaning 'to stitch songs together' (Ong 1982: 13, 59–60; *OED* 1989), a term used for the performance of oral poetry (Kirk 1985: 2; Illich and Sanders 1988: 18), is recalled. Utilitarian artefacts can assume primarily semiotic functions through visual, not auditory, tactile or olfactory, recognition: Odysseus' final journey is to be concluded when an oar is recognized as a 'winnowing fan' (Homer 750 BCd: 163), or, more literally, 'consumer of chaff' (Heubeck and Hoekstra 1989: 85). Natural phenomena can be taken as signs in their visually detectable aspects, for instance in the interpretation of omens. While the episode of Bellerophon can be regarded as the only allusion to writing in Homer, it should also be placed in the context of a rich variety of graphic signification, of deliberate semiotic constructions, and of utilitarian artefacts and natural phenomena regarded as visually significant.

Sophisticated varieties of oral discourse are also detectable. Mastery of rhetoric for public address and debate was required of Homeric heroes. Telemachus' emergence towards adult authority in *The Odyssey* is marked by his eloquence in public address (Homer 750 BCe: 44; 750 BCf: 16; Heubeck *et al.* 1988: 44). Phoenix, Achilles' tutor, educates him on a scheme which attaches comparable value to excellence in debate and in battle:

> The old horseman Peleus had me escort you, . . .
> a youngster still untrained for the great leveler,
> war,
> still green at debate where man can make their mark.

So he dispatched me, to teach you all these things,
to make you a man of words and a man of action too.

(Homer 750 BCc: 266)

Persuasiveness in debate emerges from Homer as a valued quality in the conduct of war.

The oracular pronouncements alluded to in Homer, and frequently occurring in other narratives from oral societies, can be regarded as a form of oral discourse which anticipates characteristics subsequently associated with written language. The incomplete knowledge of the Delphic oracle derived from archaeological and, primarily, literary evidence indicates that dialogue between questioner and responder normally allowed no direct sensory or visual contact between them. The priestess' voice was changed for response to enquiries. Questioning of oracular utterances was forbidden (Parke and Wormell 1956; Price 1985; Bremmer 1987; Aune 1987). Spoken oracular pronouncements therefore anticipate the impersonality and refusal of semantic ratification subsequently associated with written language. In addition, they can similarly be credited with a high degree of cognitive authority, were liable to be ambiguous and tended to be subject to close interpretation. Etymologically, the term 'exegesis', which can be glossed as recovering the meaning of written, particularly sacred, written texts, can be traced to the *exegetai*, interpreters who used to gather at the entrances to oracles and who also interpreted law and omens (Aune 1987: 86; *OED* 1989). A further similarity between oracles and writing, particularly in its early development, can be detected here – that of competence in interpretation being confined to priestly communities.

The signs frequently regarded as writing in the episode of Bellerophon are not then distinguished from coexisting forms of signification by their graphic nature, by the specialized knowledge needed for their interpretation, by the refusal of semantic ratification, or by the preservation of information over time. Other graphic or oral signs have one or more of these characteristics. The extent of the association of the writing with utterance, which is only one dimension of semiotic and communicative significance, remains uncertain, although a close reading of the episode indicates the possibility that it may have been radically silent. Where it does differ is in the transmission of information across space, without involving the memory of a human intermediary, although this was seen to have been anticipated in the Theseus legend, and in its secrecy. The secrecy is not intrinsic to the medium, as the communal participation in the inscription and recognition of lots reveals. Writing no longer appears as a radical novelty but as development from a rich variety of graphic and oral signification. Primary orality, as revealed in Homer, does not preclude elements of literacy, in the two senses of specialized knowledge required for the interpretation of oral oracular pronouncements and natural phenomena taken as signs, and of a more socially diffused requirement for mastery of public forms of oral discourse.

Oral poetry is itself a sophisticated form of oral discourse, significant to the preservation of communal information, and its informative role in primarily oral societies should be recalled (Vico 1744). To stigmatize such episodes as mythical or fictional, rather than historical, would be to import a value judgement foreign to its original context. A distinction between myth and history may not be made by cultures without written language (Goody and Watt 1963: 47). The development of history has been taken to depend on the possibility of written recording of testimony (Biber 1988: 3). Herodotus, simultaneously regarded as the 'father of lies' and the first historian, although both judgements can be tempered by a consideration of his intellectual context (Burn 1972), was concerned to ensure survival for oral traditions by collecting and transcribing them (Herodotus 430 BC: 178, 494).

In Icelandic sages, writing in the form of runes is also associated with secrecy, and the ability to interpret runes tends to be confined to a few actors in narratives. Etymologically, runes is cognate with *roun*, a secret or mystery (*OED* 1989), and runes were credited with magical power. Those unable to interpret them were vulnerable to deception: in *Egil's Saga*, a farmer's daughter had been ill and remedies had been tried:

> 'I've had runes carved,' answered Thorfinn. 'A farmer's son from near by did it, but since then she's been even worse.' . . . Egil searched the bed where she had been lying and found a whale-bone there with runes carved on it. After he had read them, he scraped them off and burnt them in the fire. . . . Then he made this verse:
>
> None should write runes
> Who can't read what he carves:

A mystery mistaken
Can bring men to misery.
I saw cut on the curved bone
Ten secret characters,
These gave the young girl
Her grinding pain.

(*Egil* 1230: 190–1)

In this episode, no oral or verbal correlate is given to the engraved or erased runes, although other episodes imply that runic forms were associated with speech. However, runes were apparently never a literary form, in the sense of being used to give form to extended discourse (Gaur 1984: 127). For instance, disputes in *Njal's Saga* over legal procedures are resolved, not by recourse to written codes, but by consulting a 'Law-speaker', who gave oral pronouncements, apparently on the basis of his memory of the law (*Njal* 1280: 306–8). Surviving examples of runes are found mainly on memorial stones or on objects such as weapons, rings and clasps (Gaur 1984: 127). From an epigraphic perspective, the substrate for these writings might cause them to be regarded as inscriptions, although some of the media are more evidently portable – amenable to transmission across space as well as pre-servation over time – than others.

Narrative examples of the use of runes for the preservation of information over time, which also reveal an association with speech, can be found. For instance, in *Egil's Saga*, runes are used to give permanence to a spoken oath:

Then he [Egil] took a horse head, set it up on the pole and spoke these formal words: 'Here I set up a pole of insult against King Eirik and Queen Gunnhild' – then, turning the horse head to-wards the mainland – 'and I direct this insult against the guardian spirits of this land, so that every one of them shall go astray, neither to figure nor find their dwelling places until they have driven King Eirik and Queen Gunnhild from this country.'

Next he jammed the pole into a cleft in the rock and left it standing there with the horse head facing towards the main-land, and cut runes on the pole declaiming the words of his formal speech.

(*Egil* 1230: 148)

Again, the substrate for inscription could be regarded, from an epigraphic perspective, as an inscription, and is used primarily for preservation over time with a deliberately fixed location in space. In the episode, the cognitive authority which is attached to a formally spoken oath is reinforced and made publicly permanent by writing. The solemnity of publicly spoken oaths persists into strongly literate cultures.

A more recent, historically documented, episode has been given fictional treatment. South American Indians carrying messages for a colonial power feared that the document would be aware of their activities:

> Two Indians take the foreman's offering to Lima in two sacks. He has given them a letter to deliver with the melons to Don Antonia Solar. 'If you eat any of the melons,' he warns them, 'this letter will tell him about it.'
>
> When they are a couple of leagues from the city of the kings, the Indians sit down to rest in a ravine.
>
> 'How would this peculiar fruit taste?'
>
> 'Must be marvelous.'
>
> 'How about trying it? One melon, just one.'
>
> '*The letter will sing*,' one of the Indians recalls.
>
> They look at the letter and hate it. They look around for a prison for it. They hide it behind a rock where it can't see anything, and devour a melon in quick bites. . . . Then they pick up the letter, tuck it in their clothing, throw the sacks over their shoulders, and continue on their way.
>
> (Galeano 1987: 140)

The phrase '*The letter will sing*' is reminiscent of the Cherokee reference to 'talking leaves' (Harris 1986: 13) and does confirm the known possibility of reading the written document to utterance.

Some common characteristics emerge from these historically disparate episodes. A broadly political interpretation of them can be illuminating. Anxieties are associated not directly with the technology of writing itself, but with the power granted to those who can interpret such message systems. Writing is also persistently associated with secrecy, mystery and death, particularly for the primarily oral actors in the narrative. In two of the incidents, writing is used for message transmission over space, deliberately bypassing the memory of the intermediary. For a modern reader, however, the living voice of orality is only known through the survival of writing over time.

The positive cultural effects of a transition from orality to literacy are difficult to determine. It has been conceded that it is difficult to isolate those cultural changes causally connected with the influence of writing (Morpurgo Davies 1986: 68–9), even in the relatively pure case of the introduction of the alphabet to Greece. Some negative effects – for instance, the disabling of the process of oral poetic performance and composition for those singers who acquire the concept of a fixed text existing prior to its instantiation in speech, associated with written language – are relatively unambiguously agreed (Lord 1960: 20, 79, 129–38; Ong 1982: 59). Later discussions (Goody 1968: 20) concede that the effects of a transition from orality to alphabetic literacy were exaggerated in studies (Goody and Watt 1963) developing from the early 1960s. They also criticize their recurrent formulations – for instance, that 'writing restructures thought' (Ong 1982; 1986) – as rather empty of specific meaning (Harris 1989). Narrative evidence, while revealing anxieties associated with the introduction of writing to primarily or strongly oral societies, also suggested that many of the characteristics associated with written language, such as its graphic nature or its inability to explain itself, were anticipated by types of signification familiar to primary orality.

One crucial cultural development, however, can be convincingly associated, both historically and causally, with the influence of written language. The historical development of logic does indicate a link with written language. Those analytic activities subsequently differentiated as formal logic and grammar markedly increase, although they do not entirely originate, with Aristotle, following the introduction of written, alphabetic language to Greece (Goody and Watt 1963). Aristotle's own term for logic is *analytika* (Goody 1977: 114) and he does not seem to make a distinction between formal logic and grammar (Ackrill 1963: 118). The removal of linguistic communication from the possibility of immediate questioning, enabled by written language, has been regarded as a prerequisite for the development of formal logic and grammar. Utterances in primary orality tend to be sponsored by individual speakers, are open to questioning, and are unlikely to be abstract sentences for analysis. Written language creates a gap between linguistic communication and reception and understanding, and, in the Western tradition, the Aristotelian syllogism is inserted there (Goody and Watt 1963; Harris 1989). The development of the gap between communication and reception had already allowed Socrates to pose the abstract question, 'What is justice?' (Harris 1989).

In this context, the causal connection between the influence of written language and the development of logic and grammar can be supported by a contrast and a continuity with features of primary orality. The practice of killing the bearer of bad news, which could be interpreted to reveal a close association between the messenger and the message, contrasts with the Socratic abstraction of assertions from their specific communicative contexts. A continuity can be detected with the analytical and exegetical activities present in primary orality, connected particularly with the interpretation of oracular pronouncements. This form of oral discourse does share the critical feature of a refusal of direct semantic ratification with written language. The exegetical activities associated with oracular pronouncements can be regarded as a precursor of the analytic activities developing with written language. Written language emerges, then, as an influence on the development of formal logic and grammar.

These preliminary considerations would suggest that Plato, and the *Phaedrus*, will have to be placed into a complex and ambivalent relation to writing and its cultural effects. The dialogue form is both mimetic of, and traceable to, oral dialectic. However, the abstract mode of reasoning has been convincingly connected with the effects of the diffusion of written language. The structural complexity of the dialogues has been alleged to be dependent for its construction and control on writing (Harris 1986), although epic poetry emerging from primary orality can be comparably complex, while remaining largely, although not entirely, self-consistent in its narrative development (Kirk 1985: 10–16). These preliminary considerations can be deepened by turning to the historical context and themes of the *Phaedrus* itself.

THE *PHAEDRUS*

The distinctions established – of written language from other forms of writing, between inscriptions and documents, and between public and private documents – can now be applied to a consideration of the historical context of Plato and of the *Phaedrus*, and to the dialogue itself. The common dimension on which they impinged, that of semantic ratification, is also crucial to Plato's preference for oral dialectic over dissemination of thought by written language.

Both writing and written language existed in Plato's lifetime (427–347 BC). Forms of writing and graphic communication existed in the Ancient Mediterranean world before the introduction of alphabetic written language to Greek territories (Morpurgo Davies 1986). For instance, in the legend of Theseus, tokens used primarily to preserve information over time occur, as well as the binary code cited, which was based on a contrast between a black and white sail for the transmission of a message over space. In one episode, Aegeus and Aethra conceive Theseus, Aegeus departs and leaves 'a sword and a pair of sandals hidden under a great rock', as tokens to be given to the child, if it is a boy. When Theseus' childhood is past, he collects the tokens, travels to Athens, and deliberately reveals the sword to Aegeus, as a clue to his identity. Recognition immediately follows (Plutarch 100: 15–20). The relation of such forms of writing and graphic communication to spoken language is not clear or agreed.

The alphabet is often taken as an example of extreme cultural diffusion from its development as the North Semitic alphabet in the first half of the second millennium BC (Goody and Watt 1963: 39; Harris 1986: 31, 109, 120; Diringer 1968, volume 1: 145–72). Evidence for alphabetic written language in the Greek mainland, islands and colonies from the mid-eighth century BC has been found (Morpurgo Davies 1986: 57). Both inscriptions and documents existed at the time of the *Phaedrus*. Many samples of early Greek writing which have survived are graffiti or other inscriptions, both in the epigraphic sense and in the related sense indicated here – that of relatively spatially fixed preservation over time (Goody and Watt 1963: 42; Morpurgo Davies 1986: 58).

The *Phaedrus* can, then, be dated as some three centuries after the beginnings of a transition from predominantly, although not exclusively, oral to oral and written communication. The particular date for composition of the *Phaedrus* is disputed, although it tends to be regarded as an early dialogue (Hamilton 1973; Harris 1989: 105–6).

The main concern of the *Phaedrus* is with written language, although diachronic filiations and synchronic similarities between written language and other forms of writing are implied. A historical link is made in a myth which attributes the invention of writing to the Egyptian god Theuth along with 'number and calculation and geometry and astronomy' (Plato 400 BCb: 96). On one interpretation, the origins of mathematics are traced to Sumer, in Southern Mesopotamia, at around 3000 BC in connection with the development of writing, although this is not to deny that Stone Age societies had elements of mathematical thought (Fauvel and Gray 1987: 43–5). The invention of geometry is tentatively traced by Herodotus (Herodotus 430 BC: 169), and more confidently by other classical sources (quoted in Fauvel and Gray 1987: 21–2) to the need to recover boundaries obliterated or altered by the rising of the Nile.

A contemporary analogy between written language and a graphic art is implied when figures in paintings are indicted for the same inability to respond to questioning as written words: 'writing involves a similar disadvantage to painting. The productions of paintings look like living beings, but if you ask them a question they maintain a solemn silence' (Plato 400 BCb: 97). In this passage also, written language is regarded as an imperfect substitute for a live speaker.

The primary concern of the *Phaedrus* is with documents, not inscriptions, and with documents further divorced from their producer by public circulation: 'once a thing is committed to writing, it circulates equally among those who understand the subject and those who have no business with it; a writing cannot distinguish between suitable and unsuitable readers' (Plato 400 BCb: 97). A contrast can be made with the role written language can assume in societies at earlier stages of a transition from predominantly oral to oral and written linguistic communication, where the ability to interpret written language is confined to particular, often priestly, communities. In episodes such as those of Bellerophon and Egil, power can be obtained by those with exclusive command of writing. Now that the ability to read is more widely shared, concern is expressed about the consequences of uncontrolled dissemination of thought by writing. Documents in written language would typically have been read aloud, perhaps by a slave (Goody and Watt 1963: 42). The immediate reader of a document would not, then, necessarily fully understand it, unless the slave were an Aesop. Attempts at direct semantic ratification would be liable to be frustrated with this form of spoken language.

Written and spoken language are extensively contrasted in the *Phaedrus*. Written language can enable information to be retained over time without immediate reliance on the memory of a human intermediary. The use of writing for the retention of information over time can weaken personal memory: 'those who acquire it will cease to exercise their memory and become forgetful; they will rely on writing to bring things to their remembrance by external signs instead of on their own internal resources' (Plato 400 BCb: 96). Writing is a 'receipt for recollection, not memory' (Plato 400 BCb: 96), only acceptable as a prophylactic against the 'forgetfulness of old age' (Plato 400 BCb: 99).

Information acquired and preserved through written language is an imperfect substitute for the knowledge developed through personal dialectic. It will fill readers 'with the conceit of wisdom instead of real wisdom' (Plato 400 BCb: 97). The possibility of direct question and answer further differentiates spoken language, particularly dialogue, from written language. If a writing 'is ill-treated or unfairly abused it always needs its parent to come to its rescue . . . it is quite incapable of defending or helping itself' (Plato 400 BCb: 97). In contrast a personal speaker can be interrogated: 'If any of them had knowledge of the truth when he wrote, and can defend what he has written by submitting to an interrogation on the subject . . . [he will] make it evident as soon as he speaks how comparatively inferior are his writings' (Plato 400 BCb: 101–2). Spoken language is, then, preferred to written language in the *Phaedrus*, particularly for the possibility of question and answer which it offers.

Forms of spoken language are also contrasted. Spoken discourse not delivered as part of a dialogue is subject to similar objections to those made to written language: 'nothing worth serious attention has ever been written in prose or verse – or spoken for that matter, if by speaking one means the kind of recitation that aims merely at creating belief, without any attempt at instruction by question and answer' (Plato 400 BCb: 101). 'Recitation' may allude to orally performed poetry and here a trace of an objection to the content of linguistic communication, not just to its form of delivery, can discerned. In the *Phaedrus* (Plato 400 BCb: 36, 81–2), and in other Platonic dialogues, rational discourse which systematically assigns the objects of discussion to agreed definitions tends to be preferred to rhetoric (Plato 395 BC) and poetry (Plato 375 BC: 130–53). For instance, poetry, which encourages immorality by presenting gods and heroes whose conduct should be imitated by the young as 'no better than ordinary mortals' (Plato 375 BC: 148), is excluded from the ideal state proposed in *The Republic*.

Dialectic speech is valued above monologue for the possibility of mutual elucidation it holds, in a letter concerned with similar themes to those of the *Phaedrus*:

> It is only when all these things, names and definitions, visual and other sensations, are rubbed together and subjected to tests in which questions and answers are exchanged in good faith and without malice that finally, when human capacity is stretched to its limit, a spark of understanding and intelligence flashes out and illuminates the subject at issue.
>
> (Plato 400 BCc: 140)

Within spoken language, then, dialogue between live speakers is preferred to rhetorical monologue. Dialogue holds the possibility of enlightenment which can only be derived from reciprocal question and answer. The feature of direct semantic ratification, which had caused written language to be seen only as an imperfect substitute for a speaker engaged in dialectic, also serves to discriminate valuable from less valued speech.

The inability to offer dialectic response seems to limit the attribution of intelligence to publicly circulated documents in written language to the appearance of intelligence. Written words seem to be intelligent: they 'appear to understand what they are saying' (Plato 400 BCb: 97), or, in another translation, 'seem to talk to you as though they were intelligent' (Plato 400 BCa: 154). Only the appearance of intelligence, and not magical powers – for instance, to cause or remove disease or to report a spoken conversation – is attributed to writing. The mystery associated with writing, plausibly connected with exclusivity of access to it, has diminished by the time of the *Phaedrus*.

A demystification of writing can also be detected in the qualification immediately imposed upon the intelligence of documents. The appearance of intelligence which written words can have is betrayed by their incapacity to adapt themselves in response to questions. If written words are interrogated, neither they nor a reader delivering them without full comprehension can exhibit the human capacity for dialectic response:

> The productions of paintings look like living beings, but if you ask them a question they maintain a solemn silence. The same

holds true of written words; you might suppose that they understand what they are saying, but if you ask them what they mean by anything they simply return the same answer over and over again.

(Plato 400 BCb: 97)

The crux of this passage warrants reiteration in an alternative translation:

written words . . . seem to talk to you as though they were intelligent, but if you question them anything about what they say, from a desire to be instructed, they go on telling you just the same thing for ever.

(Plato 400 BCa: 158)

Written words are only 'a kind of shadow' of the 'living and animate speech of a man with knowledge' (Plato 400 BCb: 98). Particularly in this formulation, the *Phaedrus* seems partly to anticipate the Aristotelian position that writing is a secondary symbolism for speech, although there are differences in emphasis: oral discourse is strongly preferred and no representative relation is implied between written and spoken forms. Documents, then, can give one behavioural sign of intelligence: they can be made to yield linguistic output. Yet their appearance of intelligence is deceptive and is betrayed by their incapacity to offer semantic ratification. They lack understanding of their linguistic output and cannot adapt it to new questions.

The degree of scepticism about the value of written language in the *Phaedrus* contrasts with the fear revealed in the story of Bellerophon and can be taken as a sign of developing intellectual maturity with regard to writing. The views given in Platonic dialogues known to be late on the value of writing are different: for instance, in the ideal state of *The Republic*, laws are to be set down in writing for dissemination and preservation (Plato 375 BC; Harris 1989: 105). If the *Phaedrus* is taken as an early dialogue, these can be regarded as subsequent changes. In Plato's time, writing would appear to be being progressively assimilated, both in historical actuality and in the political proposals of *The Republic*, into quotidian social life.

The extent of comparability between the concept of human intelligence implied by the *Phaedrus* and that implied by the Turing test is difficult to determine. A tendency to substitute considerations of intelligent behaviour for intelligence in the development of the Turing test allowed the idea of intelligence to remain poorly developed, and not necessarily self-consistent over time, in the associated discussions of artificial intelligence. The interpretation of crucial passages in the *Phaedrus* could only be further explored, and never finally explicated, by continuing to study them in relation to their coexisting semantic field. In this context, a continuity and difference between Plato and Turing can be noted. For Plato and then for Turing, intelligence is effectively equated with the faculty for arranging signs, in particular with the capacity for dialectic response. In the *Phaedrus*, and in Searle's (1980) well-known critique of the claims for computers to intelligence, without human understanding there can only be the appearance of intelligence, and not its literal presence.

CONCLUSION

The argument of this chapter can now be summarized. The supplementing of predominantly oral communication by written language may lead to apprehensions about the latter's effects, which can be plausibly connected with exclusivity of access to it. Such fears have partly diminished by the time of the *Phaedrus*. Its main concern is with the contrast between the dissemination of thought by publicly circulated documents in written language and instruction by a live speaker engaged in dialogue. Written words can only offer the appearance of intelligence without the ability to explain themselves in response to questioning.

The perspective which links documents to computers through the presence of writing and through the human faculty for constructing systems of signs can, then, illuminate the issue of the literal intelligence of computers. Historical evidence supported a logically tenable position. Claims for the intelligence of computers and of documents in written language could be seen to rest on a similar basis: that depersonalized linguistic output can be made available. Claims for the literal intelligence of computers and documents were subject to similar, although differently formulated, objections: that linguistic responses were made available without intentionality or understanding.

Scepticism about the value of a new information technology would seem to be a sign of a movement towards intellectual maturity with regard to that technology. The measure of scepticism about the value of written language in the *Phaedrus* implies that its strangeness has been partly reduced by acquaintance and that it can be considered in relation to other forms of communication. Consideration of the historical context of claims for the intelligence of computers, which reveals comparable patterns of response to novelty followed by a sceptical reaction, must be postponed until the logical operations associated with the computer have been clarified.

Chapter 4

Computers

It seems that this importance [of Turing's computability] is largely due to the fact that with this concept one has for the first time succeeded in giving an absolute definition of an interesting epistemological notion, i.e., one not depending on the formalism chosen. In all other cases treated previously, such as demonstrability or definability, one has been able to define them only relative to a given language, and for each individual language it is clear that the one thus obtained is not the one looked for.

(Gödel 1946: 84)

Logical operation signs are punctuations.

(Wittgenstein 1922: 126–7)

INTRODUCTION

On the interpretation of writing established here – that a strong connection with models in oral discourse need not be made a criterion for the recognition of writing – a computer program can then be recognized as a written artefact. To recall the previous argument: the graphic communication systems we can now regard as written languages can function as communicative substitutes for speech, although this may not have been the intention of the originators of alphabetic writing, but the possibility of replacing oral discourse is not necessary for the recognition of writing. With computer programming, we have a contemporary form of writing which seems never to have been intended as a substitute for speech. The objection that '"computer languages" are wrongly named . . . as they are *coding systems*' in the sense that they lack the ambiguity associated with written and spoken languages (Cherry 1957: 329) need not disturb the recognition of writing as linking documents in written language with programs. Designers of some programming languages would also seem to have been inescapably, although possibly unconsciously, influenced by models in written language, and by ideas of grammatical analysis, and computer programming languages may have complex connections with written languages (Leith 1990).

Apparently independently of an explicit concern with connections between documents and computers, a convincing interpretation of one sense of program has been given, which invokes criteria for communication similar to those which hold for a published text in written language: a program can be regarded, in one, although not all, of its possible meanings, as

> an ordered sequence of activities, viewable as an entity. . . . If . . . programs are to be useful, then certain logical options which can be selected according to given criteria must be testable within the processing environment itself; that is at a remove in space and time from the programmer's original conception.
>
> (Knowles 1987: 4–5)

Reception at a distance in space and time broadly corresponds to what has been characterized here as removal from direct semantic ratification, from the possibility of questioning the producer in order to clarify ambiguities.

The challenge posed by D.F. McKenzie – that of establishing a 'unifying, intellectual principle' (McKenzie 1986: 42) which would connect computers and books – has been addressed. In contrast to pre-existing written analogues to programs, the logical operations specified can now be executed by a working computer rather than simply, if even, indicated. The relative novelty of this perspective on books and computers warrants some emphasis. Distinctions between documents and computers have not been elided. On this analysis, they are both linked to, and distinguished from, each other by writing.

Such a perspective would be valuable in itself, but the analysis needs to be completed by an account of the primitive logical operations associated with the computer. Giving such an account is immediately complicated by the variety of programming languages, the heterogeneity of programs as socially produced artefacts, and the consequentially wide range of meanings acquired by the term 'program'. Real-world complexity and difficulties over definition can be avoided, without loss of generality, by recourse to automata theory. It provides models which can be correlated with a program, with data and with a computer.

AUTOMATA THEORY

Automata theory can, then, be used to provide a model for the human computational process, for programs, for data and for working computers. Its modern development can be traced from mathematical logic in the 1930s and was, at least in some respects, separate from the development and construction of working computers. Most memorably, it has been observed: 'Logic [and automata theory] was a bastard of mathematics and philosophy; while actual computers first came into being as a great feat of engineering' (Wang 1974: 292). Distinctions have tended to persist and a curious mixture of mystical practice and restrained theory has been observed (Leith 1990: 115). An integrated account of automata theory and working computers, although valuable and desirable, is not easily obtained.

A comparative, although not exhaustive, reading would also suggest that automata theory has been a partly separate activity from formal logic and mathematics, although there would seem to have been less public recognition of this contrast. The contrast also assumes a different form. In this case, there is not an easily recognizable distinction between the mathematical constructions embodied in abstract automata and the construction of a material object. Rather there is a more subtle and elusive contrast between two different modes of representation favoured by intersecting, although not unified, thought communities. Diagrammatic forms tend to be preferred for automata and notational forms for formal logic. A unified account of automata theory and formal logic, although equally desirable, remains elusive.

Three broadly distinguishable, and particularly significant, strands associated with the study of the computational process can, then, be detected: automata theory, formal and mathematical logic, and working computers. They do not seem to have been fully integrated with one another. Even texts which treat computers, automata theory and formal logic (Wang 1974; Herken 1988; Penrose 1989), or automata theory and formal logic (Davis

1958; Boolos and Jeffrey 1974), do not provide an integrated account.

The intention here is to give an exposition of automata theory and formal logic,[1] although the possibility of developing an integrated account of automata theory, formal logic and working computers will also be indicated. Although the focus will be upon automata theory, beginning with its historical development and then giving examples of significant categories of the computational process, the discussion will also explore resemblances between automata theory and formal logic, and give the model which correlates automata theory to working computers. Finally, the value of the models developed in automata studies in avoiding problems over the definition of a program, of data and of a computer will be considered.

A discussion of automata theory raises acute problems of cognitive authority and of purpose and level of exposition. Cognitive authority with regard to automata studies has tended to be implicitly claimed by discursive communities associated with mathematical logic and computer science. The question here is not with their competence within that domain but with any implied claim to exclusive proprietorship over that domain and with the extension of mathematical procedures and expectations to non-mathematical discourse. For instance, examples of computational processes tend to reflect mathematical interests while the current range of computer applications has grown beyond mathematical boundaries.

The approach here aims to respect implied claims to competence within the domain, by initially observing its required formalities, but not to concede exclusive proprietorship over that domain. With regard to automata studies, there is an apparent congruence between mathematical and ordinary discourse concepts. Discussions recognize that formal models for computability coincide in their computational power with what are regarded as intuitive notions of computability (Boolos and Jeffrey 1974: 20; Sommerhalder and Westrhenen 1988: 32–3). The central concept of automata studies – that of computability – is regarded as intuitively given and not open to formal proof (Minsky 1967: 105). More sophisticatedly, it could be regarded as culturally formed and historically developed, but still widely shared. Cultural influences for its wide dissemination might include pedagogic inculcation of methods of calculation, themselves partly associated with the exactness offered by graphic signification. Since the concern is not with the limits to mathematical formalism, examples of computational processes will be derived from a range of discourses and placed in their intellectual contexts. Computational processes primarily or, on some interpretations, only significant to mathematical formalism will be omitted, or briefly treated, with the aim of preserving clarity and concision.

Consideration of formal models of the computational process is valuable also for the insight it can yield into the semiotic aspects of the computational process, most critically in this context into the relation between graphic signification and the possibility of extensive computation. Most significantly, understanding the computational process through an abstract model can yield a grasp of fundamental matters which could never be obtained while 'immersed in inessential detail and distraction' and which can then be brought back to the practical world (Minsky 1967: 2–3). With these purposes in mind, then, attention can be turned to a more detailed consideration of significant aspects of automata theory.

Historical development

Automata have a long and complex intellectual prehistory which can only be glanced at in this context. Homer recounts that Hephaestus had constructed handmaids 'made of gold, looking like living maids . . . [with] intelligent minds, and speech too and strength' (Homer 750 BCb: 319). In Jewish legend, a golem was a human figure made from clay and other materials and supernaturally brought to life (*OED* 1989). Here an automaton is a human simulacrum. By a metaphorical extension, automaton can be used to refer to men who act, or are perceived to act, according to mechanical procedures. The history of automata as human simulacra may be one source for the analogies between the computer and the human brain. Logic machines – automata in a more restricted sense – are comparably ancient and also actual constructions, from the abacus and astrolabe, through Ramon Llull's *figura universalis* marked on concentric discs, to Jevons' logic piano and the stored program computer. The computer, as a universal information machine, has tended to displace such special-purpose information machines (Gardner 1958). The term 'robot', following Karel Čapek's play *R.U.R.: Rossum's Universal*

Robots, first performed in English in 1923, took on a range of meanings previously associated with automata and began to be used to refer to human simulacra and autonomous machines (*OED* 1989). The senses given to automata may have been consequentially restricted. An addition to the meaning of automata has been its use to refer to formalized models of the computational process.

Modern development

Automata studies, in the modern sense intended here of formal models of the computational process, can be traced to seminal papers published in the 1930s. Different definitions of effective calculability and models of the computational process were made public, by lecture or written publication, in 1935 and 1936 by Church, Kleene, Turing and Post (Church 1936; Kleene 1936; Post 1936; Turing 1937). A degree of intellectual convergence has been detected (Gandy 1988). Some direct mutual influences, for instance from Church to Post (Davis 1965: 289), are also known to have existed, although these are difficult to trace and to isolate from the embracing intellectual context, particularly with regard to purely oral exchanges. The definitions and models are considered to be equivalent in computational power.

The models of the computational process made public in 1936 were not necessarily labelled as automata at the time of their initial dissemination (Post 1936; Turing 1937). They seem rather to have emerged from a concern with formalizing the computational process and with the *Entscheidungsproblem*, that of whether there could be a general effective procedure for determining the equivalence of two well-formed formulas of a formal system. For mathematical formalism, the process of computation was analysed as consisting of the writing, erasure and substitution of symbols, according to given rules (Ramsey 1926a: 164–6). The definitions and models made public in 1935 and 1936 could be regarded as a further formalization of this analysis.

Although the different definitions and models developed by Church, Kleene, Post and Turing are acknowledged to be equivalent in computational power, there may be difficulties in encoding from one model to another. Here, then, is a trace of the difficulties which can arise from finally commensurable, but not easily compatible, notations. From the current historical perspective, the models formulated by Church, Kleene and Post can be regarded as of largely historical interest, once their formal equivalence has been noted.

The subsequent development of automata studies has witnessed a conflict between realism, in the sense of increasing resemblance between the model and working computers, and preservation of simplicity. Different models for the computational process do share a commonality of significant features. Models characteristically involve: (1) a sequence of machine or calculation states; (2) a symbol space for reading, writing and erasure; and (3) a prescribed alphabet of symbols permitted in the symbol space. The sequence of logical operations, which can include change of machine or calculation state, writing or erasing symbols, and movement with the symbol space, is determined by the current state and the symbol read. The symbol space can be either deliberately restricted or unlimited. Finite automata are accordingly distinguished from growing and from infinite automata (Minsky 1967: 13).[2] The accepted conclusion is that different models for infinite automata yield equivalent sets of computable functions (Boolos and Jeffrey 1974: 19–20). This might be explained by the commonality of significant features shared by different models, although discussions of automata seem seldom to explore this possibility. There is no limit to alternative formulations of computability. Attention can, then, be turned to the Turing machine model, thereby acknowledging the communicative value of a shared model.

Turing machine model

Turing's model for the computational process was at least partly derived from an analysis of the actions performed by a person in computing a number, or from the formalist account of this process: 'We may compare a man in the process of computing a real number to a machine which is only capable of a finite number of conditions' (Turing 1937: 231). The derivation of the model from an account of the human computational process may be one source for an unfortunate ambiguity in Turing's discussion: the sequence of states assumed by the model are referred to sometimes as states of mind and also, less anthropomorphically, as a note of instructions (Turing 1937). This inconsistency would seem to be a further possible source for the analogies between the computer and human brain or mind.

The Turing machine model for the computational process has tended to be given a dual function. First, in accord with its origin in mathematical logic, it has been used to establish the limits for mathematical formalism, although not to the exclusion of other approaches. Secondly, following the development of the stored program computer (1944), it has been used to avoid difficulties over the definition of a program and of a computer. Even when they are primarily used to avoid real-world complexity, examples of computational processes tend to be derived from mathematical or more narrowly numerical domains. Distinctions which can be made between these two uses of the Turing machine model – as a formalization of the computational process and as a means of evading difficulties over the definition of a program and a computer – are, then, analytical, not necessarily substantive. Yet each aspect deserves separate, if summary, consideration, before moving on to an exposition of the logical operations associated with the Turing machine model.

In relation to mathematical formalism, the Turing machine model has been valued for its apparently objective character. This is contrasted with the merely relative definitions which can be obtained from a formal logic. A classic statement by Gödel encapsulates this distinction (given as an epigraph to this chapter, but sufficiently significant to repeat here):

> It seems that this importance [of Turing's computability] is largely due to the fact that with this concept one has for the first time succeeded in giving an absolute definition of an interesting epistemological notion, i.e., one not depending on the formalism chosen. In all other cases treated previously, such as demonstrability or definability, one has been able to define them only relative to a given language, and for each individual language it is clear that the one thus obtained is not the one looked for.
>
> (Gödel 1946: 84)

One implied object of the contrast would be a formal system such as that of the *Principia Mathematica*, where propositions distinguished as primitive and consequent are expressed in logical notation in the object-language and in written language in the metalanguage (Whitehead and Russell 1913). The contrast made by Gödel between an absolute and a linguistically relative definition would seem since to have been largely, although not entirely, sustained. Acceptance of this dichotomy may have been one factor impeding the development of an integrated account of automata theory and formal logic. The main, although not exclusive, emphasis for mathematical formalism has tended to be on identifying domains which are not computable by purely formal procedures, rather than on the possibility of formalizing domains which remain potentially computable (Wang 1960; 1974; Herken 1988).

When the Turing machine model is used to avoid problems over the definition of a program and of a computer, there can be weaknesses in correlation from the model to working computers. The partly separate development of automata theory and working computers may be one explanation of difficulties in correlation. In particular, there may be a conflict between realism, in the sense of increasing resemblance between the model and working computers, and preservation of simplicity. Other models for the computational process, including elaborations on Turing machines which bear a closer resemblance to working computers, have been developed, but they are also more complex.

The development of Turing machine theory since 1936 seems to have been relatively unified in its themes, with a high degree of consensus on the significant features of the model, but with less cohesion with regard to notation. Each aspect – its themes, the commonality of significant features, and its notation – warrants separate consideration.

A reiterated theme of automata studies is that a process is computable if, and only if, it is Turing-machine computable, and that modifications to Turing machines do not enlarge their computational power (Davis 1958: 3; Minsky 1967: 261; Bavel 1987: 97). This has come to be known variously as Church's thesis (Boolos and Jeffrey 1974: 20), Turing's thesis (Rayward-Smith 1986: x; Shields 1987: 29) and the Church–Turing thesis (Penrose 1989: 47–9). The Church–Turing thesis will be the preferred term here. Although generally accepted, and considered not to have been falsified, it is not regarded as proven (Boolos and Jeffrey 1974: 20). It therefore provides an example of a proposition which is believed, although not considered proven, by the discursive communities claiming cognitive authority for formal logic and automata studies. Like the Turing machine model itself, it is placed outside established methods of formal proof, although there is a contrast between the treatment of the model and that of the thesis. The model tends to be regarded as an absolute account of the computational process, whereas the thesis is taken to appeal to intuition, to what would naturally be regarded as computable (Sommerhalder and Westrhenen 1988: 32).

Turing machine theory also reveals some consensus on the significant features of the Turing machine model. Significant characteristics commonly cited are: a sequence of machine states; a symbol space; and an alphabet of symbols to be accepted in the symbol space (see Figure 4.1). The Turing machine is capable of changing machine state and reading or writing symbols from the prescribed alphabet in the symbol space. The alphabet of symbols can be reduced to a binary contrast between two different symbols, or a larger number of symbols can be permitted. The most significant variable elements in the Turing machine model are, then: the number of symbols in the alphabet, the extent of the symbol space, and the number of machine states. These exist in a broadly inverse relation: a restricted alphabet of symbols requires a greater number of machine states; and a small number of machine states can be compensated for by an expanded alphabet of symbols (Shannon 1956: 157–65). A Turing machine permitted an unlimited number of machine states and an unrestricted symbol space, or a growing or infinite automaton, is considered more powerful than a machine with a restricted symbol space and a limited number of machine states, or a finite automaton. As the Church–Turing thesis implies, a restricted or expanded alphabet of symbols does not alter the computational power of the Turing machine, although it may facilitate clarity in presentation.

The set of significant features – that of a sequence of machine states, a symbol space and an alphabet of symbols – gives rise to a small, but still sufficient, set of logical operations associated with the Turing machine model. The sequence of logical operations

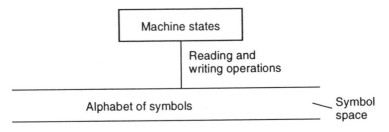

Figure 4.1 Significant characteristics of the Turing machine model

can be interpreted as a series of condition:action clauses. Each condition is composed of a combination of the current machine state and the symbol read in the symbol space. An action can consist of the symbol to be written in the symbol space, or the direction of motion within the symbol space, and the next machine state.

The graphic forms and notation given to Turing machines have been less unified than either its themes or the significant features of the Turing machine model. Forms used include diagrams, often labelled graphs (Rayward-Smith 1986) (xiii – a mathematical form of representation analogous to, although not necessarily identical with, that conveyed by the more ordinary discourse terms 'diagram' and 'flow-chart'), or notational sequences with characters drawn from a specified, although not standardized, set. The lack of a common notation has been considered to have impeded the development of automata studies (Bavel 1987: viii). A particular conflict in the notation used to represent the agreed characteristics of the Turing machine model can be between formality, as required by the discursive communities who have claimed cognitive authority in automata studies, and clarity. For instance, the notation for the sequence of states, movements within the symbol space, and symbols read and written can be reduced to a binary contrast of 0 and 1, although this does not aid intelligibility. Alternatively, comprehension can be assisted by a notation with iconic elements: for instance, a sequence of states can be designated 'q_1 q_2 q_3 ... q_n' where 'q_2 q_3 ... q_n' recall q_1 by a modified resemblance. A tension between formality and clarity is reported elsewhere in formal logic and mathematics: for instance, Whitehead and Russell concede that they have had to sacrifice notational lucidity to correctness at points in the *Principia Mathematica* (Whitehead and Russell 1913: 1). Some notations for Turing machines, together with their diagrammatic correlates, do manage to reconcile formality with clarity.

A notation which is both clear and formalized is used in a standard study of automata, *Computability and Logic* (Boolos and Jeffrey 1974), and their conventions will be adopted. Their Turing machine model, which resembles, although it does not precisely replicate, Turing's original model, is an infinite automaton: a calculating head, capable of assuming different machine or calculation states, moves above an unending tape divided into squares (see Figure 4.2). The sequence of states of the Turing machine will be represented by characters drawn from the prescribed sequence, '$q_1\ q_2\ q_3 \ldots q_n$'. The alphabet of symbols to be accepted will be limited to 0 and 1; symbols to be written will be similarly restricted; and the acts of reading and writing will be denoted as 's0' when a 0 is read or written, and 's1' when a 1 is written. No notational provision for erasure is made as this is taken to be subsumed in the act of overwriting. Symbols are read from, and written on to, the tape which corresponds to the symbol space commonly distinguished in models of the computational process. The direction of motion over the tape will be denoted by 'L' for leftwards and 'R' for rightwards moves of the calculating head. The particular Turing machine will itself be represented as a sequence of quadruples. Each quadruple is constituted by the current state of the Turing machine, symbol read, symbol to be written or direction of tape motion, and next state. A semicolon, ';', will be used to divide quadruples. The process of computation is taken to halt when no successor configuration occurs and this will be denoted by an incomplete quadruple (see Figure 4.3). In addition to these formalized elements, the following convention will be observed: at the beginning of the computation, the head of the Turing machine will be in state q_1 positioned above the left-most 1 of the input string, and, at the end of the computation it will halt over the rightmost 1 of the output string (see Figure 4.4).

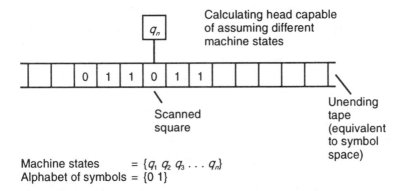

Machine states   = $\{q_1\ q_2\ q_3 \ldots q_n\}$
Alphabet of symbols = $\{0\ 1\}$

Figure 4.2 Turing machine model

Source: adapted from Boolos and Jeffrey 1974

Diagrammatic correlates to notational sequences will also be given. Once these formalities have been observed, the alphabet of symbols to be accepted will be expanded, and a degree of informality introduced, in the interests of economy and clarity.

Current state of calculating head	Symbol read	Symbol written or direction of motion of head	Next state of calculating head	
q_n	s0 or s1	s0 or s1 or L or R	q_n	

— Machine aspect

— Notational equivalent

4.3a Machine aspects and notational equivalents

$q_1 s0s1 q_n$;

4.3b Example of a complete quadruple

$q_0 s0s1$

4.3c Example of an incomplete quadruple

Figure 4.3 Notational conventions for the Turing machine

The choice and treatment of examples of the computational process is guided by the need to reflect the diverse themes already developed. Honour must be done to the development of automata studies by selecting examples of the computational process whose recurrence in the literature implies that they are significant to the subject. The concern to avoid problems of definition of a program and a computer arising from real-world complexity requires the introduction of the universal Turing machine, which corresponds to a computer. The semiotic aspects of the computational process, particularly the relation between expression and the possibility of constructing meaning, remain of interest. Semiotic considerations have also guided the presentation here, which attempts to reconcile the potentially conflicting requirements of formality and clarity. The concern is not with the limits to mathematical formalism, and the content of examples of

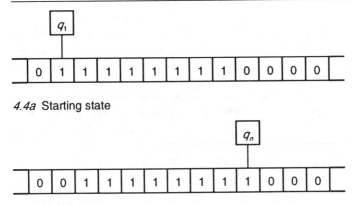

4.4a Starting state

4.4b Halting state

Figure 4.4 Turing machine starting and halting states

the computational process is accordingly derived from a range of discourses rather than predominantly from complex mathematical discourse.

Examples of computational processes illustrating four significant categories developed in automata studies will, then, be given to clarify the computational power of the Turing machine model: (1) a deterministic numerical calculation; (2) a deterministic taxonomic process; (3) a non-deterministic Turing machine which can then be recast as a deterministic Turing machine; and (4) the universal Turing machine. A commentary will be given after each example on aspects of interest specific to that procedure and, after the set of examples, on the Turing machine computations as a whole.

Determinism and non-determinism

The frequent recurrence of allusions to determinism and non-determinism in the literature of automata studies would seem to be indicative of their significance to models of the computational process. Determinism and non-determinism can be controversial topics and there is a significant distinction between the senses which tend to be prescribed for use with regard to Turing machines and the meanings they can obtain in wider discourse. In discussions of Turing machines, determinism and non-determinism are given precise and technical senses. Concisely, although not fully, defined, a deterministic Turing machine is one in which there is only one sequence comprising symbol to be written, next state following from any given state, and symbol read. In contrast, for a non-deterministic Turing machine, there can be more than one such sequence following from a given state and symbol read. Even within automata studies, although there tends to be a consistent contrast between determinism and non-determinism, non-determinism can become more complex and acquire associated meanings.[3] In wider discourse, determinism and particularly non-determinism can carry a more extensive range of meanings: for instance, non-determinism can be associated with intuitive thought or reasoning involving probability. The terms can be come multivalent to the extent of being vacuous.

Failing to distinguish between the precise technical senses that determinism and non-determinism are given when applied to Turing machines and their wider discourse meanings can be a source of confusion. In this respect, the situation is analogous to that already encountered with regard to information: in information theory, and specifically in *The Mathematical Theory of Communication* (Shannon and Weaver 1949), information was seen to be given a precise and technical definition, which deliberately excluded any connection with meaning; in wider discourse it could carry a wider range of senses, and confusion between these senses and its deliberately restricted definition could occur. In the discussion to follow, determinism and non-determinism are to be taken in their technical senses, unless otherwise indicated.

A deterministic numerical calculation

The deterministic numerical process to be exemplified will be that of multiplying in monadic notation, where each '1' signifies a numerical unit (Boolos and Jeffrey 1974: 53). The numbers to be multiplied, A and B, are each represented as unbroken strings of 1s, on an unending tape otherwise marked 0, and are separated from each other by a single 0. The following conventions will be observed. The Turing machine will begin in state q_1 scanning the leftmost 1 of A. The result will also be given in monadic notion: the Turing machine will halt scanning the rightmost 1 of the string of 1s taken as the result (see Figure 4.5).

The task can be simplified by analysing it into plausibly effective components. B can be shifted $(A - 1)$ times along the tape; then, when this is complete, the blank tape from B's original

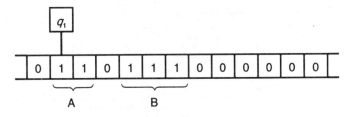

4.5a Starting state

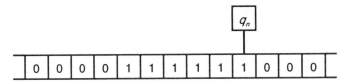

4.5b Halting state

Figure 4.5 Turing machine for multiplying in monadic notation

leftmost 1 can be filled up with 1s until a single string is completed; the Turing machine head must then proceed to the rightmost 1 and halt. Each component can then be represented as a distinct procedure which is connected to other procedures: first a counting procedure, based on A, to control the number of iterations for shifting B (the computational process should start with this procedure); secondly, a shifting procedure for B; thirdly, a procedure to return to the counting procedure; and, finally, a halting procedure which includes filling the tape with 1s from B's original leftmost 1. A diagram may make this sequence more intelligible (see Figure 4.6).

Each procedure must then be analysed into a larger number of discrete steps corresponding to the operations permitted by the Turing machine model. For instance, the counting procedure can begin by replacing the 1 read with a 0 and changing state. A move right is then made and, at this point, a choice is made: if a 1 is read the count is not over and a transition to the shifting procedure must occur; if a 0 is read the count is over and a transition to the halting procedure is made. Whenever there is only one 1 in A, the Turing machine will transfer to the halting procedure. Other procedures have similarly to be analysed into the small set of

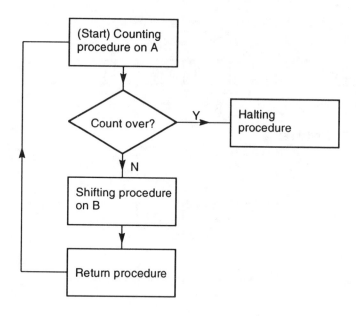

Figure 4.6 Diagram for multiplying in monadic notation

available operations, although it would be tedious to enumerate them. The complete procedure is given as a diagram, resembling a labelled graph (with annotations to correlate it with the previous diagram indicating distinguishable procedures), as a sequence of quadruples, and as a grid (see Figure 4.7).

Aspects specific to this task warrant commentary. There is a degree of choice in constructing the process and there may be a conflict between notational clarity and economy, even when the notation is strictly formalized. At each stage in the procedure, there is a binary possibility for the next procedure, depending on whether a 0 or 1 is read. When procedures are aggregated together, transitions between aggregated procedures remain reducible to binary divisions. The process is not fully reversible in the sense that input strings cannot be unambiguously reconstructed from the output string: for instance, given the final string '1111', it cannot be determined whether the input strings were '1' and '1111' or '11' and '11'.

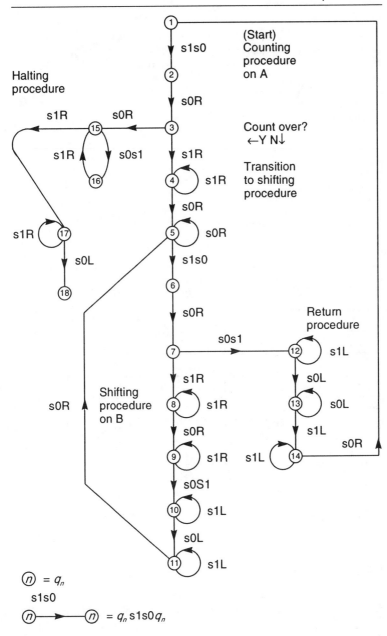

4.7a Flow-chart

Figure 4.7 Turing machine for multiplying in monadic notation

q_1s1s0q_2; q_2s0Rq_3; q_3s0Rq_{15}; q_3s1Rq_4; q_4s0Rq_5; q_4s1Rq_4; q_5s0Rq_5;
q_5s1s0q_6; q_6s0Rq_7; q_7s0s1q_{12}; q_7s1Rq_8; q_8s0Rq_9; q_8s1Rq_8; q_9s0s1q_{10};
q_9s1Rq_9; q_{10}s0Lq_{11}; q_{10}s1Lq_{10}; q_{11}s0Rq_5; q_{11}s1Lq_{11}; q_{12}s0Lq_{13}; q_{12}s1Lq_{12};
q_{13}s0Lq_{13}; q_{13}s1Lq_{14}; q_{14}s0Rq_1; q_{14}s1Lq_{14}; q_{15}s0s1q_{16}; q_{15}s1Rq_{17};
q_{16}s1Rq_{15}; q_{17}s0Lq_{18}; q_{17}s1Rq_{17}; q_{18}

4.7b Sequence of quadruples

State	q_1	q_2	q_3	q_4	q_5	q_6
Input						
0		Rq_3	Rq_{15}	Rq_5	Rq_5	Rq_7
1	s0q_2		Rq_4	Rq_4	s0q_6	

State	q_7	q_8	q_9	q_{10}	q_{11}	q_{12}
Input						
0	s1q_{12}	Rq_9	s1q_{10}	Lq_{11}	Rq_5	Lq_{13}
1	Rq_8	Rq_8	Rq_9	Lq_{10}	Lq_{11}	Lq_{12}

State	q_{13}	q_{14}	q_{15}	q_{16}	q_{17}	q_{18}
Input						
0	Lq_{13}	Rq_1	s1q_{16}		Lq_{18}	
1	Lq_{14}	Lq_{14}	Rq_{17}	Rq_{15}	Rq_{17}	

4.7c Grid

Figure 4.7 (Continued) Turing machine for multiplying in monadic notation

A deterministic taxonomic process

The example of a deterministic taxonomic process to be given is adapted from the Linnaean taxonomy for the horse (Linne 1792; Donovan 1820). The input data will indicate whether a differentiating characteristic is, or is not, present in the object for classification. A 1 will indicate the present of the specified characteristic and a 0 its absence. The Turing machine will accept the input and produce a taxonomy of the object. A degree of informality in expansion of the Turing machine alphabet, and limitation on the range of input data, will be introduced in the interests of economy and clarity. The process is presented as a taxonomic table, as a taxonomic tree, and in informal Turing machine notation (see Figure 4.8).

Some aspects of this taxonomic process again deserve commentary: first, in relation to historical antecedents in formal logic; secondly, in comparison with its contemporary intellectual context; and, thirdly, in connection with the possibilities offered by graphic communication.

From a historical perspective, the diagram can be seen to resemble the tree of Porphyry (Bochenski 1961: 134–5). Labels

Differentia	Input	Output
A heart with two auricles and two ventricles. The blood is warm and red. The lungs respire regularly alternate. The jaws are horizontally incumbent on each other.	1 0	Class: Mammalia. Not in this taxonomy.
Hoofed feet. Fore-teeth in both jaws.	1 0	Order: Belluae. Have obtusely truncated fore-teeth. Their motions are slow and heavy. They live on vegetable food, from which their digestive organs draw a tincture without dissolution Not in this taxonomy.
Has six parallel, erect, fore-teeth above, and six, which project a little, in the lower jaw; one short tusk, distant from the other teeth on each side of both jaws. The female has two teats in the groin.	1 0	Genus: Horse – *Equus.* Not in this taxonomy.
Has solid hoofs.	1 0	Species: *Equus caballus* or Common horse. Species: Chilean horse. Obscure species said to have cloven hoofs.

4.8a Taxonomic table

Figure 4.8 A deterministic taxonomic process

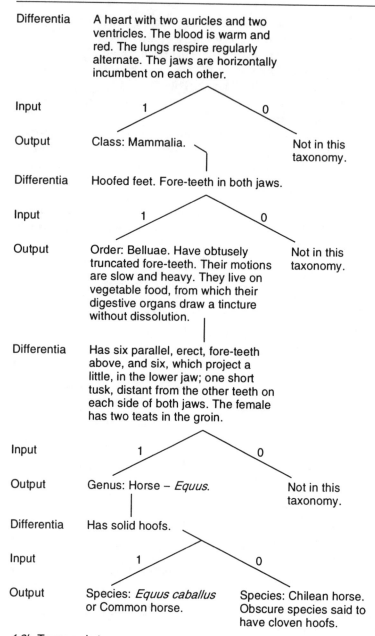

Differentia — A heart with two auricles and two ventricles. The blood is warm and red. The lungs respire regularly alternate. The jaws are horizontally incumbent on each other.

Input — 1 / 0

Output — Class: Mammalia. — Not in this taxonomy.

Differentia — Hoofed feet. Fore-teeth in both jaws.

Input — 1 / 0

Output — Order: Belluae. Have obtusely truncated fore-teeth. Their motions are slow and heavy. They live on vegetable food, from which their digestive organs draw a tincture without dissolution. — Not in this taxonomy.

Differentia — Has six parallel, erect, fore-teeth above, and six, which project a little, in the lower jaw; one short tusk, distant from the other teeth on each side of both jaws. The female has two teats in the groin.

Input — 1 / 0

Output — Genus: Horse – *Equus*. — Not in this taxonomy.

Differentia — Has solid hoofs.

Input — 1 / 0

Output — Species: *Equus caballus* or Common horse. — Species: Chilean horse. Obscure species said to have cloven hoofs.

4.8b Taxonomic tree

Figure 4.8 (Continued) A deterministic taxonomic process

q_1s1s{Class: Mammalia.}q_2;
q_1s0s{Not in this taxonomy.}
q_2s1s{Order: Belluae. Have obtusely truncated fore-teeth. Their
motions are slow and heavy. They live on vegetable food, from which
their digestive organs draw a tincture without dissolution.}q_3;
q_2s0s{Not in this taxonomy.}
q_3s1s{Genus: Horse – *Equus.*}q_4;
q_3s0s{Not in this taxonomy.}
q_4s1s{Species: *Equus caballus* or Common horse.}
q_4s0s{Species: Chilean horse. Obscure species said to have cloven
hoofs.}

4.8c Informal Turing machine notation

Figure 4.8 (Continued) A deterministic taxonomic process

Source: adapted from Linne 1792

could be given to nodes of the tree and they could be differentiated in a hierarchy from genus to species. Such labels are not
essential to the computational process. Analogously, in discussions of formal logic and classification, genera have been viewed
as constructions not real existents. They may still be regarded as
useful constructs. Classically in formal logic – for instance, for
Aristotle (Aristotle 323 BCa: 5–7) and Porphyry (Bochenski 1961:
134–5) – genera and their differentia are predicated of species,
although species and their differentia are not predicated recipro-
cally of genera. One example given by Aristotle, and comparable
in content to the taxonomy described here, is concerned with the
implication of existence between the genus 'animal' and the
species 'fish': 'if there is a fish there is an animal, but if there is an
animal there is not necessarily a fish' (Aristotle 323 BCa: 40).

The genus:species relation tends to be commonly cited in
formal logic. The relation from species to genus is also familiar as
class inclusion. It is sometimes acknowledged that class inclusion
can be interpreted as material implication when propositions
rather than classes are denoted by the variables of formal logic
(Bell 1937, volume 2: 491). On one interpretation, which is implicitly endorsed here, elaborations on class inclusion are dismissed
as verbal fictions. For instance, 'q characterizes a' is regarded as a
lengthened verbal form of 'a is q', which does not add to its
meaning (Ramsey 1925: 38).

In relation to its contemporary intellectual context, the

taxonomic process can be compared both to a semantic network and to a thesaurus. The idea of a semantic network is generally traced to Quillian's model of semantic memory (Quillian 1968), although antecedents to this have been adduced (Gardin 1973). Semantic memory was to be modelled as a mass of nodes inter-connected by associative links. The form given to subsequent semantic networks has shown a significant reduction in complexity. A consensus seems to have emerged on a small set of relations – for instance, of part–whole and distinguishing properties (Johnson-Laird 1988: 52) – which can be seen to correspond to the classic distinctions of genus, species and differentia. From a historical perspective, the reduction in complexity could be regarded as an assimilation of a computational process to estab-lished taxonomic and logical structures. It could also be taken as empirical confirmation of the observation that elaborations on class inclusion can be regarded as verbal fictions.

From the perspective of information retrieval, the genus: species relation can be seen as analogous to the BT:NT hierarchies familiar from thesauri. J.-C. Gardin showed that other indexing vocabularies could be described as lexicons with relations be-tween terms of the lexicon reducible to binary predicates of the form Ri(xy). In the expression, Ri(xy), x and y are to be under-stood as terms from the indexing vocabulary and Ri as the relation between them: for instance, the index entry 'animal *see also* fish' could be rendered as 'R*see also*(animal fish)'. The relation Ri could be either uninterpreted or variously labelled, but still remained reducible to class inclusion (Gardin 1973).

The taxonomic process described could also be regarded as tautological in the sense that the conclusion is unambiguously implied by the input data. Yet with less narrowly circumscribed universes of discourse, the conclusion might not be self-evidently readable from the input. Procedures may become so complicated that their results cannot be known with certainty prior to the analysis. Analysis itself can be subject to error. If formal logic is taken to consist of tautologies, its propositions may never sur-prise us (Wittgenstein 1922: 165), but they need not have been fully anticipated.

Graphic representation both allows the construction of the taxonomy and possibly makes it deceptive. In reading the dia-gram, a convention is implicitly invoked by which it is read from top to bottom. A similar progression is generally, although not universally, observed in reading written language. Yet, at the same time the appearance of clarity and rigour offered by the diagram can be deceptive. The clarity of the graphic representation may obscure difficulties in initial formulation of categories and subsequent assignment of objects of discourse to agreed categories. Darwin, for instance, found the concepts of classification and species problematic rather than self-evident (Darwin 1859: 108, 456). Categorizations, even once agreed, do not unambiguously determine assignment decisions and there may be a legitimate degree of freedom in choice of assignments.

A non-deterministic Turing machine

The term 'non-determinism' has tended to be used in two distinguishable senses with regard to Turing machines. First, in its apparently earlier and more technical sense, it is used to refer to machines where there is more than one continuation specified from a given machine state and input: the machine can then either halt, until moved by an input either randomly generated or from an external operator, or choose between different continuations. There can be some ambiguity over whether a non-deterministic Turing machine which chooses from different configurations is only a mathematical fiction or a potentially constructible automaton. Secondly, by analogy, non-determinism is also used to refer to non-deterministic machines recast as deterministic Turing machines.

In its technical sense of a machine which chooses between different configurations, the idea of non-determinism can be traced to Turing's 1936 paper which alludes to, although it is not greatly concerned with, choice machines, which halt in an ambiguous configuration until moved by a choice from an external operator (Turing 1937: 131–2). In an extension of this technical sense, the notion of non-determinism has also become associated with automatic modification of the original parameters of a Turing machine. This concept tends to be traced to McCullough and Pitts' work on neural networks published in 1943 (Minsky 1967), but can also be discovered in Turing's 1948 and 1950 papers, where it is called machine learning (Turing 1948; 1950). The proposed process of learning by punishment and reward is also reminiscent of the Utilitarian, particularly Benthamite, pleasure–pain calculus (Bentham 1780).

The issue of non-determinism can be clarified by recasting a non-deterministic Turing machine as a deterministic Turing machine. A further degree of informality, particularly with regard to the precise specification of sub-procedures and in presentation as diagrams, not quadruples, will be introduced, for the purposes of clarity and economy of exposition.

The example to be given will be a process for ascertaining whether two words are synonymous or not. Various criteria for synonymy have been proposed, not always distinguishing between spoken and written language. Some discussions concede that the only final test for synonymy is inter-substitutability in all contexts while remaining acceptable to competent interpreters of that language. The existence of full synonymy has also been disputed. From a semiotic perspective, which insists on difference as the source of meaning, full synonymy is unlikely except as a symptom of structural change, of a shift in the distribution of meanings (Saussure 1916: 118, 162). In this context, attention is focused upon written language and the criterion for synonymy to be employed approximates to inter-substitutability. Synonymy is to be determined by whether a word can be substituted for another in a full, although not necessarily entirely exhaustive, list of collocations derived from the *Oxford English Dictionary* (*OED* 1989). This work, although no longer current, can still be regarded as a valuable if imperfect register of the use of words in written English. Two words, furze and gorse, will be supplied, together with a set of contexts for each, and words will be matched against alternative contexts to test whether they are synonymous. A degree of liberty has been taken over the delimitation of a word and the terms, although closely related, are revealed not to be equivalent.

Non-determinism can be exemplified in two distinguishable senses in this process. First, the series of contexts can be presented in the form, 'context1 or context2 or . . . context*n*', and a random choice made between them (see Figure 4.9a). This can then be recast as a deterministic progression from context1 to context2 to . . . context*n* (see Figure 4.9b). Secondly, the Turing machine can halt at the point of decision as to whether or not a substitution is legitimate, for the decision to be made by an external operator who compares it with the set of contexts provided (see Figure 4.9c). This element of non-determinism can then be recast as a deterministic matching against the set of legitimate collocations (see Figure 4.9d). Although both types of non-determinism can be recast as an identical deterministic process, a significant contrast emerges from the recasting. The first type of non-determinism, involving random choice of temporal priority among contexts, is more clearly recastable without a reduction of confidence in judgement; the second, appealing to human judgement of legitimate substitutability, will remain equivalent only if the external operator limits the comparison to the prescribed set of collocations. If this condition is observed, both deterministic and non-deterministic Turing machines arrive at the same halting state, given the same set of input data (see Figure 4.9e).

The consensus of automata theory is quite clear: that a non-deterministic Turing machine cannot compute anything which is not computable by a deterministic Turing machine (Sommerhalder and Westrhenen 1988: 211–19). Technically, a deterministic Turing machine can be regarded as a restricted non-deterministic Turing machine for which there is only one sequence following from a given state and input (Rayward-Smith 1986: 76; Sommerhalder and Westrhenen 1988: 219). Discussions suggest that non-determinism is only significant, and then in the sense of a non-deterministic Turing machine recast as a deterministic Turing machine, when issues of speed or efficiency of computation are in question. The examples given here supported the theme of the equivalence in computational power of deterministic and non-deterministic Turing machines, by showing that non-deterministic processes could be recast as deterministic computations. They could also be regarded as illustrating the consensus that expanding the Turing machine alphabet does not enlarge the computational power of the Turing machine, although it may enable greater clarity in exposition.

The universal Turing machine

The aim of this section is to recall the historical origin of the universal Turing machine; to clarify its distinction from special-purpose Turing machines; to indicate the diversity of possible constructions for the universal Turing machine; and to describe one such construction. In the description of a construction for the universal Turing machine, a diagrammatic description, together with a verbal account of its significant features, will be given. Finally, the elusive notion of a universal machine will be discussed.

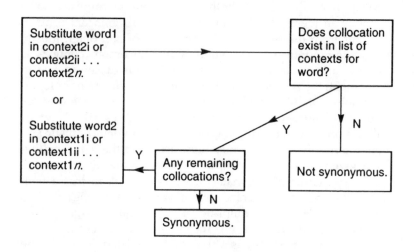

4.9a Non-deterministic procedure for determining synonymy

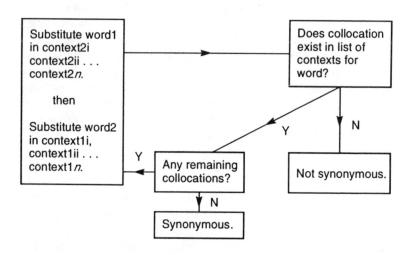

4.9b Recasting of non-deterministic procedure for determining synonymy as a deterministic procedure

Figure 4.9 Non-deterministic and deterministic procedures

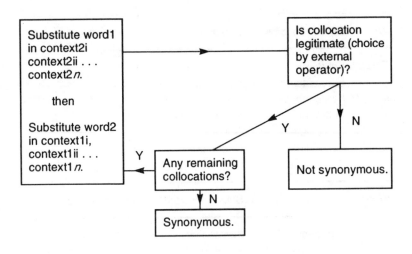

4.9c Non-deterministic procedure for determining synonymy

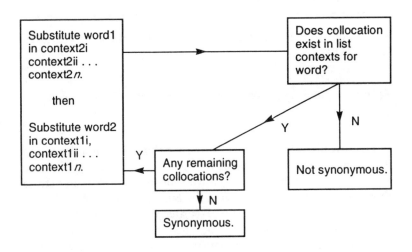

4.9d Recasting of non-deterministic procedure for determining synonymy as a deterministic procedure

Figure 4.9 (Continued) Non-deterministic and deterministic procedures

Word1	Collocations given	Substitute word2	Legitimate collocation
Furze	Furze–chat	Gorse–chat	Y
	Furze–chirper	Gorse-chirper	N
	Furze–chucker	Gorse–chucker	N
	Furze–hacker	Gorse–hacker	N
	Furze–kite	Gorse–kite	N
	Furze–lark	Gorse–lark	N
	Furze wren	Gorse–wren	N

Word2	Collocations given	Substitute word1	Legitimate collocation
Gorse	Gorse–chat	Furze–chat	Y
	Gorse–duck	Furze–duck	N
	Gorse–hatch	Furze–hatch	N
	Gorse–hatcher	Furze–hatcher	N
	Gorse linnet	Furze linnet	N
	Gorse–thatcher	Furze–thatcher	N

4.9e Example of two words which would be determined not to be synonymous

Source: *OED* 1989

Figure 4.9 (Continued) Non-deterministic and deterministic procedures

Historically, the universal Turing machine was first described in Turing's 1936 paper, as an extension of the Turing machine formalization. In that context, it was constructed to demonstrate that there could be no solution to the *Entscheidungsproblem* (Turing 1937), which, as was explained earlier in this chapter, can be glossed as whether there could be a generally effective procedure for determining the equivalence of two well-formed logical formulas. With the subsequent development of the stored program computer (1944), the universal Turing machine has been given significance for reasons not anticipated in its origin. In particular, it has been used as a model which can be substituted for the stored-program computer in order to avoid problems in definition over a computer: where, for instance, can a definite boundary be drawn between a computer and its peripherals for storage and display, or between hardware and software?

There is a substantial commonality, as well as a significant difference, between special-purpose Turing machines and the universal Turing machine. First, the commonality can be noted: the universal Turing machine is itself a Turing machine with a similarly restricted set of computational operations – erasing and writing symbols, movement within the symbol space, and changes of machine state. Secondly, the significant distinction can be indicated: the universal Turing machine will precisely imitate the actions of a particular Turing machine in transforming input to output data. The very existence of the universal Turing machine, as an abstract mathematical construct, has itself been taken as a testimony to the thesis that any computational process can be modelled as a Turing machine (Minsky 1967: 136; Davis 1988a: 158–9).

There can be a lack of clarity in the literature with regard to the distinction between a special-purpose Turing machine and the universal Turing machine. Difficulties in the definition of the universal Turing machine are apparent from an early stage in the development of automata theory. It has been argued that a universal Turing machine needs to be encoded in a simple form – that there would be little value in claiming universality for a Turing machine which required an excessively complex encoding of a Turing machine computation (Davis 1956: 167) A special-purpose Turing machine alone is sufficient for exemplifying many computational processes. Accordingly, in some (Davis 1958; Boolos and Jeffrey 1974), although not all (Minsky 1967; Herken 1988), discussions of computability, it has received more attention than the universal Turing machine.

Understanding of the commonalities and distinction between a special-purpose and the universal Turing machine can be clarified by further consideration. For special-purpose Turing machines, a restricted or expanded alphabet was permitted, although expanding the alphabet of symbols accepted did not enlarge the machines' computational power. Similarly, details of encoding and representation can differ for the universal Turing machine. Again, there can be a conflict between strict formality and clarity. Economy in the construction of a universal Turing machine – for instance, reducing the number of machine states to a minimum –

can also conflict with clarity and intelligibility in exposition (Minsky 1967). Different special-purpose Turing machines could be specified to perform identical tasks. Similarly, it is possible to construct different universal Turing machines to perform equivalent tasks of imitation. The universal Turing machine is, then, distinguished from special-purpose Turing machines by its universality, but, in other respects (such as the set of primitive operations, liberty in constructing machines to perform equivalent tasks, and a potential tension between formality or economy and intelligibility), it is similar to special-purpose Turing machines.

Different constructions for the universal Turing machine, of differing levels of complexity, intelligibility and economy, are possible (Minsky 1967). Expositions given in the literature of automata studies embody, and sometimes comment on (Minsky 1967), the diversity of possible constructions. The presentation here will be limited to one construction for the universal Turing machine and to an indication of essential procedures in that construction. A more detailed and formalized exposition than that given here might obscure, not clarify, essential procedures and concepts.

The universal Turing machine is required to simulate exactly the behaviour of a special-purpose Turing machine whose description is supplied in a suitably encoded form. To preserve continuity, the conventions of sequences of quadruples used in the preceding exposition of Turing machines will be retained. The theme of automata theory – that modifications to the alphabet of symbols accepted does not affect the computational power of the Turing machine model – implies that a reduction of the sequence of quadruples to a binary string would be possible. However, reduction of quadruples to a binary sequence would not assist intelligibility in exposition. Data, as distinct from machine quadruples, can continue to be presented as a binary string of 0s and 1s.

In order to simulate the behaviour of a special-purpose Turing machine, the universal Turing machine must be presented with a description of the Turing machine to be imitated and the data on which it is to operate. The initial tape for the universal Turing machine must, therefore, include a description of the Turing machine and its data (see Figure 4.10a). In the particular method of construction employed here, the current quadruple of the Turing machine to be imitated is copied to a specified portion of the tape of the universal Turing machine and a space must be reserved on the tape of the universal Turing machine for it (see Figure 4.10b).

The essential procedures required to replicate the behaviour of the Turing machine specified are: to consult the Turing machine description; move to the appropriate point in the data; carry out the specified operations on the data; return to the Turing machine description and locate the next quadruple. The process then begins again and is continued until no further quadruple is specified by the Turing machine description, at which point it halts, in accord with the formalities previously established (see Figure 4.10c). Some more technical additions are required to implement these procedures: the position reached in the data must be temporarily marked, overwriting the data, and the temporary marker erased on return to the data and the data overwritten restored; the

Turing machine description $\{q_1s1s0q_2; \ldots q_n\}$	Turing machine data {0 1}	

4.10a Essential information on tape for the universal Turing machine

Space reserved for copying current quadruple	Turing machine description $\{q_1s1s0q_2; \ldots q_n\}$	Turing machine data {0 1}	

4.10b Initial tape for the universal Turing machine

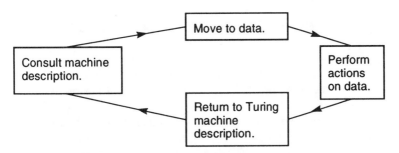

4.10c Essential procedures for the universal Turing machine

Figure 4.10 Schema for a universal Turing machine

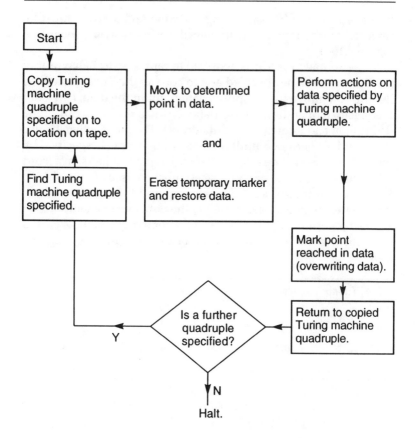

4.10d Procedures for the universal Turing machine further analysed into sub-procedures

Figure 4.10 (Continued) Schema for a universal Turing machine

current quadruple of the Turing machine imitated must be copied to a reserved position on the tape of the universal Turing machine and then overwritten by the next quadruple specified. These additional procedures can be regarded as sub-procedures of the enveloping procedures of moving to the appropriate point in the data and consulting the Turing machine description (see Figure 4.10d). The universal Turing machine can begin by searching for the quadruple beginning q_1 and will halt when the Turing machine imitated would halt, that is when no succeeding quadruple is specified. The binary string of transformed data on the tape of the universal Turing machine is taken to be the result of the computation.

The methodology of construction used here has been analytic rather than synthetic: beginning with essential procedures and analysing these into sub-procedures. Detailed description of those sub-procedures would have added to the complexity of the construction, possibly obscuring rather than facilitating an understanding of the distinction between a special-purpose and the universal Turing machine. For the universal as for the special-purpose Turing machines, a small set of primitive operations – writing, reading, and movement within the symbol space – is sufficient to construct complex procedures.

The notion of a universal machine seems itself elusive and insubstantial. Like a chameleon, the identity of a universal machine merges into its context. Curiously, and almost anomalously, for logic with its insistence on the axiom of identity (Leibniz 1686: 87; 1716: 206–22), a universal machine is a construction which is only valued when it is, in one sense, not identical with itself, when it is transformed by accepting the description of a special-purpose Turing machine. Even those closely connected with the development of computing can find the idea of universality implausible or difficult to grasp (Davis 1988a: 152–9): a remark from 1956 can exemplify this:

> If it should turn out that the basic logics of a machine designed for the numerical solution of differential equations coincide with the logics of machine intended to make bills for a department store, I would regard this as the most amazing coincidence that I have ever encountered.
>
> (Howard Aiken quoted in Davis 1988a: 152)

An understanding of the distinction between a special-purpose and the universal Turing machine and of the, admittedly difficult, notion of a universal machine can help explain this coincidence.

A contrast with familiar special-purpose information machines may further clarify the idea of a universal machine. Special-purpose information machines, such as an abacus, astrolabe or typewriter, are designed for a specific task, or a variety of related tasks. In contrast a universal information machine can be programmed to imitate any such special-purpose machines. The contrast has been wittily explored by transposing the distinction to industrial machines:

> As machines computers, unlike all other products of the industrial revolution, are neither task-specific nor are they dimension-specific. You cannot use a lawnmower to shave, and they make a disappointing means of transport. The computer is a universal machine which can be adapted to an infinite number of tasks.

(Alston 1988: 173–4)

The elusiveness and apparent difficulty of the concept of a universal machine would seem to be matched only by its simplicity once grasped.

To summarize, the idea of a universal information machine emerged from a concern with establishing the limitations of purely formal procedures in mathematics and was later adapted to serve also as a model for working computers. The distinction between a special-purpose and the universal Turing machine was not always emphasized or fully clarified in the relevant literature. It could be obscured by technical details which, although they might be formally required in some contexts, do not assist clarity in exposition. The universal Turing machine is itself a Turing machine. The set of primitive operations familiar from the construction of special-purpose Turing machines is, as the Church–Turing thesis implies, sufficient for the construction of the universal Turing machine. Different constructions for the universal Turing machine were possible. The notion of a universal information machine may initially appear complex and implausible but should be perceived as simple once understood.

Commentary

Some aspects of these computational processes deserve commentary: first, from a semiotic perspective concerned with the relation between the form and content of sign systems; and, secondly, glancing at the relation between the methodology employed in the construction of these diagrammatic forms and that more familiar from formal logic, anticipating themes which will be more fully developed in the next section of the chapter on the relation between automata theory and formal logic.

Semiotic aspects

Mathematics is often cited as the paradigm case of a discipline whose conceptual development has been critically dependent on the possibility of graphic representation (Harris 1986: 152). The relation between mathematics and graphic representation holds true even at an elementary level (Goody 1977: 12). Similarly, even in computational processes of such limited scope, a human calculator rapidly becomes a prisoner of the notation. At a more sophisticated and complex level, Whitehead and Russell remarked (given as an epigraph to the Introduction but again sufficiently significant to bear repetition):

> Various collocations of symbols become familiar as representing important collocations of ideas; and in turn the possible relations – according to the rules of the symbolism – between these collocations of symbols become familiar, and these further collocations represent still more complicated relations between the abstract ideas. And thus the mind is finally led to construct trains of reasoning in regions of thought in which the imagination would be entirely unable to sustain itself without symbolic help.
>
> (Whitehead and Russell 1913: 2)

Whitehead and Russell continue: 'Ordinary language yields no such help' (Whitehead and Russell 1913: 2).

A more radical position can be developed from this supplementary observation: that not only does ordinary language, whether written or spoken, not yield help to mathematics, but ordinary written language is not a prerequisite for the development of mathematics. Historically, sophisticated mathematical notations have been developed without a coexisting script which can confidently be identified as phonetic, for instance in Mesopotamian mathematics (Goody 1968: 21). In contrast, the growth of formal logic was seen to be historically associated with the development of written language and its inability to explain itself in response to questioning.

Formal logic seems to be less frequently cited as a form of discourse critically dependent on the possibility of graphic representation. Yet the thesis of Whitehead and Russell – that mathematics is reducible to logic – would seem to imply that their comments on the value of symbolism are equally applicable to formal logic as well. An observation on the significance of notation to logic was made by Wittgenstein in the *Tractatus Logico-philosophicus*: 'It now becomes clear why we often feel as though "logical truths" must be "postulated" by us. We can in fact postulate them in so far as we can postulate an adequate notation' (Wittgenstein 1922: 163). Although this remark is analogous to Whitehead and Russell's comments on the value of specialized symbolism to mathematics and logic, there is also a significant contrast: Whitehead and Russell seem, although only in part, to regard notation as something objectively given, analogous to the discovery of the Platonic universals denoted; Wittgenstein rather emphasizes the human construction of the notational artefact. The notational systems constructed are intolerant of errors, and vulnerable to collapse if modified:

> The introduction of a new expedient in the symbolism of logic must always be an event full of consequences. No new symbol may be introduced in logic in brackets or in the margin – with, so to speak, an entirely innocent face.
>
> (Wittgenstein 1922: 123)

The origin of logical systems as human artefacts does not, then, necessarily imply that they can be fully understood even by their immediate makers.

Written language has itself been associated with mathematics, in the sense of number, calculation and geometry. The origins of mathematics were seen earlier (p. 58) to be traceable to Southern Mesopotamia, at around 3000 BC, in connection with the further development of writing (Fauvel and Gray 1987: 1–45). Similarly, in the myth of the origin of writing recounted by Plato in the *Phaedrus*, the invention of writing was ascribed to the Egyptian god Theuth, who also invented number, calculation, geometry and astronomy (Plato 400 BCb: 96). Some notations for number, such as the Roman symbolism, have used alphabetic characters rather than the more clearly differentiated Arabic numerals. Translating from an unfamiliar to a known written language, with the aid of a grammar and a dictionary, can give rise to patterns similar to those reported by Whitehead and Russell in developing mathematical logic: particular collocations tend to recur and their repetition reinforces the recognition that they represent possible paths to a final expression.[4] It is difficult not to recall again Bacon's apothegm: 'Writing [maketh] an exact man' (Bacon 1597: 209).

Methodology of construction

The method of elaboration of the Turing machine model from its concise formulation seems to have been anticipated in Vico's comments on the geometric method:

> The whole secret of the geometric method comes to this: first to define the terms one has to reason with; then to set up certain common maxims agreed to by one's companion in argument; finally, at need, to ask discreetly for such concessions as the nature of things permits, in order to supply a basis for arguments, which without some such assumption could not reach their conclusions; and with these principles to proceed step by step in one's demonstrations from simpler to more complex truth, and never to affirm the complex truths without first examining singly their component parts.
>
> (Vico 1725: 125–6)

For Vico, geometry and arithmetic differed only in the quantities they treated, not in their methods (Vico 1710: 156). Where Vico would differ significantly from Gödel's (1946: 84) emphasis on the objective character of the Turing machine model is in his insistence on the humanly constructed nature of any concise formulation, as well as its further elaboration, rather than receiving such models as objects of contemplation. An analogy can be drawn with the contrast between Whitehead and Russell's implicit suggestion that a notation is objectively given and Wittgenstein's emphasis on its postulation.

The notion of logical form needs to be simultaneously invoked and questioned. It needs to be invoked in order to establish that notational sequences and diagrams are mutually equivalent. Similarly, alternative models for the computational process could be said to be equivalent in computational power. A corollary to form, interpretation, has also to be invoked to distinguish numerical from taxonomic processes. Here, then, we have an exemplification of Boole's aim in the *Laws of Thought*, of processes of reasoning whose verification depends solely on their form and which are distinguished from each other by their interpretation, not their form (Boole 1854: 37–8).

A rigid notion of logical form, in which ideas are taken to exist prior to and independently of the means for expressing them, has already been implicitly questioned in the attention given to the role of symbolism in enabling thought. It can be further questioned when difficulties in inter-semiotic encoding and translation are noted. Encoding between notational and diagrammatic forms may not be easy, even when it can be reduced to a formal process. Translating notational or diagrammatic forms into verbal, and then oral, correlates may involve distortion or a loss of clarity. The idea of logical form, although it remains indispensable analytically, can be deceptive if it is allowed to obscure discernible connections between a notation and the possibility of expressing meaning.

A relation to the connectives of formal logic is implicit, rather than explicit, in the Turing machine model. The most frequently occurring transition rule determining changes between states would seem to be strongly analogous to material implication in formal logic. For example, the Turing machine quadruple 'q_1s0s1q_2', could be read, with its interpretation preserved, as material implication in formal logic, '$(q_1 \wedge s0) \rightarrow (s1 \wedge q_2)$'. It is perhaps unfortunate the Turing machine model should implicitly recall the logical connective which has been, both historically and in contemporary practice, simultaneously the most vexed and the most productive. It may be recalled that material implication can be read as 'If . . . then', but that difficulties in interpretation have tended to follow (Quine 1937: 84; and see p. 36). Similarly the state transition rule for Turing machines can be read as 'If . . . then' (Johnson-Laird 1988: 161–2), but, unless this is deliberately restricted to an informal reading, comparable difficulties in interpretation are liable to follow.

The overprinting of symbols is reminiscent of the formalist account of the computational process, and plausibly derived from or at least influenced by it. For mathematical formalism, it should be recalled, the process of computation was regarded as consisting of the writing, erasure and substitution of symbols, according to given rules (Ramsey 1926a: 164–6). The replacement, in Turing machine computations, of one symbol by another from the given alphabet also recalls Wittgenstein's remark that: 'The method by which mathematics arrives at its equations is the method of substitution' (Wittgenstein 1922: 171).

These implicit connections to formal logic do hint at the possibility that the Turing machine model, rather than being received solely as an absolute account of the computational process, can also be read as an alternative formulation for formal logic. A remark from the *Tractatus Logico-philosophicus* may again be relevant: 'A particular method of symbolizing may be unimportant, but it is always important that this is a possible method of symbolizing' (Wittgenstein 1922: 59). From this perspective, the Turing machine model could be regarded as analogous to the primitive formulations of formal logic.

LOGIC

In contrast to the relative thematic unity of automata theory, formal logic is less unified, in both its historical development and modern practice. One history of formal logic opens with the remark that 'apart from "philosophy" there is perhaps no name of a branch of knowledge that has been given so many meanings as "logic"' (Bochenski 1961: 2). A continuity of analytic temperament, and a reluctance to trust to intuition, is admitted. Traces of such a temperament, insistent on consistency and intolerant of ambiguity, can be discerned in the tendency for logicians to obscure the diversity of logic and to present interpretations as if they were agreed accounts of a monolithic field.

The historical development of formal logic and grammar was seen to be associated with the introduction of written language to Greek territories, and, plausibly, connected with its influence, particularly the removal of linguistic communication from direct semantic ratification. The origins of modern logic are often traced (Russell 1903: 10) to Boole's *An Investigation of the Laws of Thought*, first published in 1854. Modern logic tends to be distinguished from previous logic by its more extensive use of notational symbols and mathematical methods. It has no sharp boundary which can be used to demarcate it from mathematics and, in contrast to the apparently intuitive plausibility of the Turing machine model, can be forbiddingly technical in character. The notation of modern symbolic logic is also complex and varied. Modern logic, then, is not cohesive in either its themes or notation. Automata theory tended to draw on mathematical logic – for instance, when formalizing the Turing machine model – and to give examples of computational processes derived from mathematical domains.

A degree of consensus in modern logic is discernible with regard to the logical operators, although their application has changed historically, even since Boole (1854). It seems to be generally agreed that the logical operators ($\wedge$, $\vee$, $\sim$, $\rightarrow$, $\leftrightarrow$) are sufficient for the development of formal logic. They appear to be commonly regarded as functionally complete in the sense that to add further operators could only yield statements logically equivalent to ones already expressible with the given operators. Precisely delimited senses are prescribed for their use in formal logic and with reference to automata, which are not necessarily coincident with the senses their verbal correlates (and, or, not, if . . . then, if, and only if . . . then) can obtain in ordinary written or spoken discourse.

It also seems to be agreed that the logical operators can be derived from more concise primitive formulations. For Whitehead and Russell in the first edition of the *Principia Mathematica*, published in 1913, it was to some extent (although not entirely) arbitrary which two logical operators were to be taken as primitive. ~ and $\vee$ were treated as the primitive operators and $\sim p$ and $p \vee q$ taken as primitive expressions (Whitehead and Russell 1913: 1–7). The *Tractatus Logico-philosophicus*, published in 1922 and following developments in symbolic logic since the *Principia Mathematica*, implicitly appeals to the concise expression $\sim p \wedge \sim q$ (Wittgenstein 1922: 15). It also offers a more satisfying account of the status of such concise formulations and asserts that 'the proper general primitive signs are not "$p \vee q$", "$(x).fx$", etc., but the most general form of their combinations' (Wittgenstein 1922: 125–7). In the introduction to the second edition of the *Principia Mathematica* (published in 1925) '$p|q$', to be read as $\sim p \vee \sim q$, is introduced as the primitive idea (Whitehead and Russell 1913: xvi). Other primitive formulations have been proposed (Bochenski 1961: 411–12).

Disagreement is marked upon the legitimate scope of a symbolic logic. One strong Anglo-American philosophical tradition has been to insist that ordinary discourse can be, and for analytical purposes should be, reduced to symbolic logic. For instance, in the *Principia Mathematica*, no distinction is made between contradictions expressible in the logical symbolism, such as the famous paradox connected with the class of all classes which are not members of themselves, and those which arise solely in connection with the discourse about that symbolism (Whitehead and Russell 1913; Ramsey 1926a). Subsequently, a distinction was made between logical and semantic contradictions in the *Principia Mathematica* (Ramsey 1926a). The distinction was later rephrased as a distinction between the object-language of a symbolic logic and the metalanguage of discourse about that logic. It has been widely, although not universally, accepted by those working in the analytic tradition developed by Russell (Kneale and Kneale 1962: 664). The analytic method is exemplified, although not solely represented, by logical positivism (Ryan 1988: 33) which tended to insist on analysing discourse until determinate sense was reached (Ayer 1936). The practice of logical translation – the reduction of sentences in ordinary language into notational forms – which tends to be used by introductions to logic (Copi 1953; Delong 1970; Hodges 1977; Lemmon 1965; Newton-Smith 1985) reveals a similar insistence.

Significant objections to the reduction of ordinary discourse to formal logic can be found. Isaiah Berlin, for example, argued that logical translation rested upon fallacies which had persisted from their 'earliest beginnings in Greek philosophy' and which still obsessed 'many distinguished philosophers'. It involved the belief that a logically perfect language, free from the ambiguities and supposed inadequacies of ordinary discourse, could be invented or discovered. Meaning, for both ordinary language and symbols in logical sentences, tended to be conceived as a simple correspondence between symbols and a reality known independently of language. Yet the development of language was to a large extent the growth of metaphors, not of literal usage, and metaphors could be sources of genuine illumination. Logical translation could still have some benefits, however, for instance in encouraging rigour of thought (Berlin 1950).

More radical limitations of the useful scope of formal logic were indicated by F.P. Ramsey, who drew an incisive distinction between logic as a symbolic system and logic as the analysis of thought. In a critique of the *Principia Mathematica*, Ramsey stated:

These two meanings of 'logic' are frequently confused. It really should be clear that those who say mathematics is logic are not meaning by 'logic' at all the same thing as those who define logic as the analysis and criticism of thought.

(Ramsey 1926a: 184)

This distinction was subsequently further developed. Formal logic was concerned 'simply to ensure that our beliefs are not self-contradictory' (Ramsey 1926b: 87). In non-mathematical and non-scientific domains, it was not even clear that consistency was always beneficial: 'human logic or the logic of truth . . . is not merely independent of but sometimes actually incompatible with formal logic' (Ramsay 1926b: 87). The dominant philosophical tradition was acknowledged: 'In spite of this nearly all philosophical thought about human logic and especially induction has tried to reduce it in some way to formal logic' (Ramsey 1926b: 87–8).

Descartes' assertion that the

> long chains of reasoning, quite simple and easy, which geometers are accustomed to using to teach their most difficult demonstrations, had given me cause to imagine that everything which can be encompassed by man's knowledge is linked in the same way.
>
> (Descartes 1647: 41)

would seem to be an influential source for the attempt to assimilate human reasoning to a mathematical or logical model. Similarly, John Stuart Mill argued that 'nearly the whole, not only of science, but of human conduct, is amenable to the authority of logic' and tried to reduce induction to formal logic (Mill 1843: 9, 283–638).

The distinction between formal and human logic seems to have acute contemporary significance. Increasingly, computers are being used for applications in human or social, not primarily mathematical or scientific, domains. Yet, in conformity with the strong analytical tradition, attempts have been and continue to be made to reduce discourse about social or human matters to symbolic logic (Leith 1986a; 1986b; 1990; Sergot 1988). Discussions of automata may occasionally acknowledge that the primitive operations associated with the computer are as much logical as mathematical. Yet, even if this is conceded, a further distinction must be made between logic as a symbolic system and logic as the analysis of thought.

A logical procedure

An example of a logical procedure from Dickens' *Hard Times* (Dickens 1854) – a text published in the same year as Boole's *Laws of Thought* – which remains an incisive critique of attempts to reduce the richness of ordinary discourse to logical patterns, will help substantiate the distinction between formal and human logic.

'Bitzer,' said Thomas Gradgrind. 'Your definition of a horse.'

'Quadruped. Graminivorous. Forty teeth, namely twenty-four grinders, four eye-teeth, and twelve incisive. Sheds coat in the spring; in marshy countries, sheds hoofs, too. Hoofs hard, but requiring to be shod with iron. Age known by marks in mouth.' Thus (and much more) Bitzer.

'Now girl number twenty,' said Mr Gradgrind. 'You know what a horse is.'

(Dickens 1854: 5–6)

No direct allusion to Boole can be detected in this particular passage, although traces of other figures representative of a logical temperament can be discerned. Bitzer's abrupt telegraphic style seems to mimic the terse and laconic prose developed by Linnaeus for defining natural genera and species (B.D.J. 1911: 733). The definition does resemble the Linnaean taxonomy for the horse adduced earlier to exemplify a deterministic computational process. It is difficult to escape an allusion to Mill in Gradgrind's name or not to recognize similarities between the education of the Gradgrind children and that later revealed by Mill – 'never was a boy; never played at cricket' (quoted in Williams 1958: 55) – in his *Autobiography* (Mill 1873).

Bitzer's definition of a horse can be translated into a logical statement. For instance, the following logical statement could be derived, with the definition implicitly abbreviated:

If, and only, if ([quadruped] and [graminivorous] and [has forty teeth]) then horse.

The logical statement can also be represented, in a diagrammatic form, as a binary tree (see Figure 4.11). The taxonomy given in the figure could also be read as an indication of similarities between logical procedures and models of the computational process. In form, as well as content, the taxonomy, derived from a logical statement, is strongly analogous to the deterministic taxonomic process illustrated earlier and could itself be transformed into a Turing machine computation.

The diagram is beginning to appear as a curious graphic form, possibly containing both scriptorial and pictorial elements. In this instance, the diagram is, in some sense, isomorphic with the logical statement. The statements and diagram could be said to share the same logical form. Such taxonomic diagrams have already

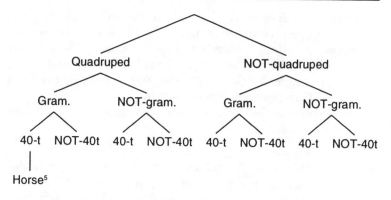

Figure 4.11 A logical procedure
Source: after Dickens 1854: 5–6

been seen to resemble the simplified semantic networks associated with, and partly derived from, Quillian's model of semantic memory (Quillian 1968). The initially more complex model of semantic memory does seem to have been partly reduced to a method for giving diagrammatic form to logical statements (Charniak and McDermott 1985: 22–3; Johnson-Laird 1988: 328–9).

The strong indications of the relative failure of attempts to reduce discourse about social and human affairs to symbolic logic for the purposes of computation – for instance, in the development of logic programming for expert systems (Leith 1990) – seems to testify to the significance of the distinction of human from formal logic. It should be noted, however, that there is nothing about the computer itself (as distinct from some of the research communities connected with computing, themselves influenced by received traditions of logical analysis) which commits us to a reduction of ordinary discourse to symbolic logic.

Object-language

Even given the significance of the distinction of human from formal logic, a critic might accept an imperfect obligation at least to indicate the account of the object-language endorsed. An account which is, in some sense, congruent with the consensus of automata theory, and which would help make explicit the analogies already indicated between automata theory and formal logic, seems to have strategic value in encouraging their integration. It should be recalled that a comparative reading suggested that automata theory and formal logic had been, in part, separate developments. For Gödel (1946: 84), and for subsequent commentators, the Turing machine model provided an absolute account of the computational process whereas definitions in formal logic were inescapably linguistically relative.

An interpretation of formal logic analogous to the consensus of automata theory does exist, developed in the 1920s prior to the formalization of the computational process, and apparently not yet integrated with Turing machine theory. For Wittgenstein in the *Tractatus Logico-philosophicus* (Wittgenstein 1922), if we begin with the truth functions of atomic formulas, then to whatever extent we generalize upon them, we never reach propositions significantly different from those atomic truth functions. This interpretation of formal logic is congruent with the consensus of automata theory, that modifications to the Turing machine model do not enlarge its computational power. The account of formal logic which can be derived from the *Tractatus Logico-philosophicus* was subsequently explicated (Ramsey 1923; 1925; 1927) and extended to mathematics (1926b) by Ramsey, particularly in 'The foundations of mathematics' (Ramsey 1926a).

On this interpretation of the object-language, and in brief, the predicate calculus is collapsed into the propositional calculus. The universal quantifier is treated as a conjunction whose writing cannot be completed and the existential quantifier as an uncompleted disjunction. For instance, $(x).fx$ would be regarded as equivalent to $(fx_1 \wedge fx_2 \wedge fx_3 \ldots fx_n)$ and $\exists x.fx$ as equivalent to $(fx_1 \vee fx_2 \vee fx_3 \ldots fx_n)$. The only difference, on this interpretation, between the propositional and predicate calculus is:

> that, owing to our inability to write propositions of infinite length, which is logically a mere accident, $(\phi).\phi a$ cannot, like $p.q$, be elementarily expressed, but must be expressed as the logical product of the set of which it is also a member.
>
> (Ramsey 1926a: 204)

The indispensable notational advantages following from the introduction of the quantifiers for unwritten conjunctions and disjunctions are still conceded.

Such an interpretation of formal logic could be rendered more persuasive, and an integrated account of formal logic and automata theory obtained, if the contrast made by Gödel between an absolute formulation and a relative definition could be dissolved. It could then be replaced by a recognition that both automata theory and formal logic are socially constructed, and historically specific, modes of discourse. The particular contrast between the diagrams used in automata theory and the notational forms developed in formal logic could then be transformed into a finally arbitrary distinction along a continuum from iconic to scriptorial signs, with no absolute epistemological authority attached to either mode of representation. The intention, then, is to preserve the forms of automata theory and of formal logic, while reconciling their interpretation.

Gödel's comments on the absolute nature of Turing's model of the computational process can be read to recall themes inherited from Aristotle and Plato. For Plato, knowledge was founded on recollection of the ideal forms of ideas which existed prior to being known (Plato 385 BC: 130–54). Analogously, the model for the computational process is not regarded as a historically specific and humanly made construction, but as the discovery of an absolute idea. Aristotle regarded the perceptible as existing prior to perception, and as unaltered by the act of perception (Aristotle 323 BCa: 21, 43). A diagram, then, as a sensible, visual object can be granted absolute status. Yet the notion of absolute perception of ideal forms, existing independently of their knowers, has been increasingly questioned in the philosophy of science, the sociology of knowledge, and semiotics.

The distinction between an absolute definition and one tied to a particular formalism has been questioned in the philosophy of science. Kuhn in *The Structure of Scientific Revolutions* began to 'suspect that something like a paradigm is prerequisite to perception itself' (Kuhn 1962: 113). Aristotle and Galileo looked at swinging stones, and the first saw constrained fall, the second a pendulum: 'The alternative is not some hypothetical "fixed" vision, but vision through another paradigm, one which makes the swinging stone something else' (Kuhn 1962: 113; also 113–28). Fleck in *Genesis and Development of a Scientific Fact*, alluding to the curious nature of diagrams, poised between the evidently conventional system of writing and the seemingly more natural iconicity of aspects of the pictorial, asserted: 'There is no visual perception except by ideovision and there is no other kind of illustration than ideograms' (Fleck 1935: 141). With regard to mathematical and logical constructions, concern must be focused on perception by social subjects, not personal or biological individuals. The same personal and biological individuals have been members of the intersecting discursive communities concerned with automata theory and formal logic. The absence of a fully integrated account would seem to testify to Fleck's observation that 'the stylized uniformity of his [an individual's] thinking as a social phenomenon is far more powerful than the logical construction of his thinking' (Fleck 1935: 110). Acceptance of a dichotomy between an absolute formulation and a relative definition may also have been a factor inhibiting the development of a unified account. Yet, if the notion of innocent perception is rejected, this dichotomy can no longer be sustained.

The illusory nature of absolute perception, and the inter-subjective construction of reality, have also been emphasized in the sociology of knowledge. For Berger and Luckmann in *The Social Construction of Reality*, reality was socially constructed and mediated. Spoken and written language, and other sign systems, were inter-subjective experience rendered objective. Symbolic universes, broadly corresponding to the idea of a paradigm or thought community, were social products with a history. To understand their meaning, one had to understand the history of their production. Such symbolic universes did not have significant existence unless they were sustained by the beliefs of the agents involved in their construction and reproduction (Berger and Luckmann 1966: 85–142). Even if symbolic worlds are perceived in reified terms, they remain humanly made artefacts. The emphasis on the inter-subjective construction of symbolic universes contrasts with the Platonic idea of recollection of ideal forms existing before being known, and not influenced by the act of knowing, and the Aristotelian emphasis on the perceptible existing apart from the act of perception.

Semiotics offers a way of recasting, and refining, the distinction made by Gödel between an absolute formulation and a relative definition into a contrast between types of sign. In some, although not all, semiotics, as for Fleck and Kuhn in the philosophy of science, it has become increasingly difficult to conceive of innocent perception without semiotic mediation, of signifieds existing independently of a sign-system. The sign-system through which perception is mediated need not be purely verbal or reducible without loss of distinctions to verbal language. The diagram has already emerged here as a curious graphic form, mixing, and often combining, iconic and notational elements. A specifically semiotic distinction – that of iconic from scriptorial signs – can be used first to isolate the contrast between automata theory and formal logic, and then to integrate the two discursive activities by suggesting that the distinction is better understood as a contrast along a continuum between types of sign, not as a dichotomy between a natural process and a deliberately constructed formalism.

The distinction between iconic and scriptorial signs can be recalled. Both are constituted by a contractual, not natural, relation between a signifying and signified aspect. For an icon, there is a resemblance between signifier and signified: the signifier is motivated by the signified. In contrast, for scriptorial signs, the connection between signifier and signified is arbitrary or unmotivated. Scriptorial signs, particularly written language, are often closely associated with speech, whereas iconic signs may not be given verbal or oral correlates. Yet although this contrast may be one historical source for a harsh distinction of the scriptorial from the iconic, it will only partially serve to discriminate them. Rather, they can be discriminated along a continuum within the graphic, from motivated or analogical to an arbitrary or unmotivated connection between signifier and signified.

The notion of the autonomous existence of proofs, not vivified by the beliefs of a thought community, can, then, no longer be accepted. The particular contrast between an absolute or natural formulation and a relative definition has also to be dissolved. In this case, it could be recast as a contrast along a continuum from iconic to scriptorial. The elements of motivation in the Turing machine model may be one source for its being accepted as natural. That model can now be regarded as a mathematical construction, with a specific historical origin. The distinction between the apparently absolute model of the computational process associated with the Turing machine formulation and the more clearly conventional models of formal logic has been recast as a more satisfactory distinction between predominantly iconic and scriptorial forms. An account of formal logic congruent with the consensus of Turing machine theory has thereby been rendered more persuasive.

CORRELATION FROM AUTOMATA TO WORKING COMPUTERS

The task of fully integrating automata theory with the study of working computers still remains. Difficulties in integration seem to arise from the partly separate historical development of automata theory and working computers and also from those problems of definition, connected with historical change and social complexity, which recourse to automata theory avoids. The aim here is only to indicate the correlation which does exist from the Turing machine model to working computers, and the difficulties of integration.

A clear correlation from the abstract model for the computational process to working computers can be indicated. The Turing machine corresponds to a program; the binary string of the Turing machine alphabet read from and written on to the tape corresponds to input and output data; and the universal Turing machine corresponds to a computer (Shannon and McCarthy 1956: vii; Boolos and Jeffrey 1974: 54; Weizenbaum 1976: 63; Aleksander 1984: 71; Davis 1988a: 166, 171; Penrose 1989: 24, 56–7). For automata theory, where the issue is discussed, it tends to be a matter of definition that the computer or universal Turing machine is transformed into, or precisely imitates, the particular Turing machine specified by a program (Weizenbaum 1976: 68–105; Rayward-Smith 1986: xi; Aleksander and Burnett 1987: 32–6; Penrose 1989: 51–6): 'each new program makes the computer into a new machine' (Bolter 1984: 39). Earlier it was suggested that the literature of automata studies could betray a lack of clarity on the distinction of the universal Turing machine from special-purpose Turing machines and that, in some discussions of the computational process, the special-purpose machines had tended to receive more attention than the universal one. Similarly, although the transformation of the computer or universal Turing machine into the special-purpose Turing machine specified by a program can be clearly stated, it is not always emphasized.

From the point of view of a concern with the relation between writing and computers, a program, like a Turing machine, remains a written construction; the machine configuration specified by a program is considered equivalent to the written program by automata theory; data, unlike the Turing machine alphabet, need not be written; and the written construction represented by a universal Turing machine is replaced by the artefact of the computer as machine.

The exactness obtainable from writing and other forms of graphic signification seems to have been an essential preliminary to the construction of computers as machines. It should be recalled that the construction of working computers and the development of automata theory had been, in part, separate developments. Formal logic and mathematics, from which context automata theory emerged, have been revealed as strongly dependent on graphic representation for their development. It is also plausible that without the exactness encouraged and enabled by writing, and the systematic control of complexity obtainable from writing and other graphic forms, such as diagrams, the physical artefact of the computer could not have been constructed. In contrast to the citation of mathematics as a discipline critically dependent on the possibility of graphic representation, the importance of writing and graphic signification to the construction of computers as machines seems to have received little notice. The development of logic and systematic methods of enquiry and analysis has been recognized as an essential precursor to their construction: 'without the systematic analysis that Boolean methods make possible, the construction of large-scale digital computers would be virtually unthinkable' (Davis 1988b: 319). This is an isolated remark whose implications are not fully explored. However, it does indicate that writing, and particularly the exactness associated with writing, could constitute a crucial element linking the development of mathematics, formal logic and automata theory to the construction of the computer as machine.

The correlations from models of the computational process to programs, data and computers could not have been fully anticipated at the time of the original formulation of the Turing machine model, or of the other contemporary models for the computational process, and some potential weaknesses in the correlations can be detected. For instance, although a special-purpose Turing machine corresponds to a program and its alphabet to data, this correlation may be difficult to establish precisely in working practice. With the Turing machine model, there was extensive choice in constructing Turing machines to perform equivalent tasks. The potential heterogeneity of programs, as socially produced artefacts, is liable to be equally, if not more, unrestrained. In particular, the distinction between a program and a collection of data can become arbitrary.

While computing practice has changed and continues to change, automata theory has given a relatively stable model, both over time and for contemporary discourse. In historical terms, the Turing machine model has remained relatively constant while computer materials and architecture have been altered. For contemporary discourse, a single, although not notationally unified, model of the computational process enables an enquirer to bypass the difficulty of determining directly the significant commonality shared by the multiplicity of programming languages, and to evade real-world problems connected with the definition of a program. A fully integrated account must traverse those very problems of change and complexity whose evasion makes automata theory valuable.

CONCLUSION

What conclusions, then, can be drawn with regard to the value of the Turing machine model? Its value, both over time since it was made public in 1936 and since the subsequent development of working computers, and for contemporary discussion, seems to lie in its inter-subjectivity rather than its apparent objectivity. It has enabled those interested in computing to avoid problems arising from the definition of a program, the complexity and multiplicity of programming languages, and historical changes in computer materials and architecture.

In its current development, automata theory has certain limitations connected with restrictions on its inter-subjective scope. Automata theory emerged in the context of formal logic and mathematics, and in particular from a concern with the limitations of purely syntactic procedures in computation, although it does not appear to have been fully integrated with formal logic. In this chapter, the possibility of an integrated account has been indicated. The Church–Turing thesis provides an apposite example of a proposition which is accepted, but not considered proven, by the standards of those discursive communities that have claimed cognitive authority in automata studies. Even when the Turing machine model is formalized, there can be a conflict between formality and clarity. In contemporary terms, interest in computational operations has spread beyond the specialized re-search communities from which automata theory, formal logic and working computers emerged. Other discursive communities have different, and arguably equally valid, criteria for discussion and proof. The Turing machine model could retain its strategic value as a common referent point for those interested in compu-tational operations, although it need no longer be credited with absolute epistemological status.

The relevance of this chapter to the main theme of the book should be recalled. Documents and computers are unified, and differentiated, by writing. The development of formal logic can be plausibly connected with the influence of the use of written language, particularly its removal from direct semantic ratifi-cation. The logical operators which govern the transformation of information inputs to information outputs by a computer were already present in ordinary written language, and, with carefully delimited senses, in formal logic. Distinctions between docu-ments and computers have not been obscured. In contrast to pre-existing written analogues to programs, the logical operations of a program can now be executed by a working computer rather than simply, if even, indicated.

Chapter 5

Intelligence of computers

[Teiresias] had revealed to men what they ought not to know.
(*Encyclopaedia Britannica* 1911a)

INTRODUCTION

Speculations on the possibility of computers displaying intelligence are often traced to Alan Turing's paper, 'Computing machinery and intelligence', first published in 1950. It introduced a test for computer intelligence, subsequently known as the Turing test, which required the convincing simulation of human linguistic responses to questions. Claims for the literal intelligence of an appropriately programmed computer were publicly challenged in 1980 in an article by John Searle, 'Minds, brains and programs'. In this context, the qualification '*literal* intelligence' is again used to distinguish the substance of intelligence from its appearance alone, and 'intelligence' is used to cover both aspects, unless otherwise indicated. For Searle, even an adequate simulation of intelligence would still lack intentionality, 'that feature of certain mental states by which they are directed at or about objects or states of affairs in the world' (Searle 1980: 419–24). For Searle, then, it is a matter of definition that literal intelligence must involve a human act of interpretation, and this position is endorsed here. Searle's criticism of claims for the literal intelligence of computers has been widely (Motzkin and Searle 1989), although not universally, accepted. Claims for the possibility of the adequate simulation of intelligence, as distinct from its literal presence, by an appropriately programmed computer are now also increasingly, although not entirely, subdued (Michie 1988; Churchland and Churchland 1990).

The thesis developed here represents a departure from an immediate analogy between the computer and the human brain or mind. A perspective which links computers directly with documents through writing and through the human faculty for constructing socially shared systems of signs has been established. From such a viewpoint, it can be shown that: claims for the literal intelligence of an appropriately programmed computer, in the tradition following from the Turing test, have rested on a similar basis to claims for the intelligence of a document, the production of depersonalized linguistic output; and that claims for the intelligence of computers and documents are subject to an identical objection, that such linguistic output is made available without a prior act of comprehension by the artefact. Such a position would be tenable on purely logical grounds, but it is also supported by historical evidence.

The possibility that intelligence was attributed to documents in the transition from oral to oral and written linguistic communication in Ancient Greece has already been discussed. The aim of this chapter is to place speculations for computer intelligence and the development of the Turing test in their intellectual and historical context.

INTELLIGENCE OF COMPUTERS

Speculations on the possibility of computer intelligence were preceded by the construction of abstract models for the computational process. Turing's 1948 and 1950 papers followed the construction of universal logical computing machines. They also introduced the possibility that computers could be programmed to perform tasks which would be called intelligent when performed by humans. Various games, including chess, the learning and translation of languages, cryptography and mathematics were proposed as possible fields of endeavour. The idea of modification of the original parameters of a program was also introduced. This was called machine learning and an analogy between the computer and the brain was made explicit. Changes in the machine configuration were compared to the development of the originally unorganized cortex of the human infant (Turing 1948; 1950). More recent research into neural networks (Ford 1989) seems to represent a revival of interest in this approach (Sloman 1983). Perhaps because of the partly separate development of automata theory and working computers, some discussions tend to leave it unclear whether neural networks can be assimilated to the Turing machine model (Ford 1989; Sloman 1983). In the previous chapter, an allusion was made to neural networks in the course of a discussion of non-deterministic automata and, in particular, of automatic modification of the original parameters of a Turing machine. In the context of automata theory, neural networks have been considered equivalent in computational power to finite automata (Minsky 1967: 32–6).

The Turing test itself was introduced by 'Computing machinery and intelligence' (Turing 1950). The test required the simulation of human linguistic responses to questions. Conditions were established which would make it impossible for the human enquirer to obtain sensory evidence as to whether the responses emanated from a person or a computer. For instance, answers were preferably to be typewritten rather than handwritten or spoken, in order to remove personal traces from the linguistic output. If the questioner was deceived by the simulation, the Turing test would have been passed. Computers could then be credited with showing intelligent behaviour. The production of depersonalized linguistic output was thus to be taken as an adequate indicator of intelligence (Turing 1950). Subsequent research in artificial intelligence, and speculations that computers might either be intelligent or made to exhibit intelligent behaviour, have by no means confined themselves to attempting to meet the Turing test, although it has been influential (Searle 1980; Motzkin and Searle 1989). However, clarity and generality can be obtained by confining attention primarily to the Turing test, and this will be done here.

Connections can be made from the Turing test to Turing's personal situation. The primary deception considered by Turing, not necessarily followed in the subsequent development of the Turing test, involved a disguise of gender. First a man and a woman were to be hidden from the enquirer and to attempt to give replies which would mislead the questioner into believing that the man was the woman. Then, the man was to be replaced by a computer. If the computer was as deceptive as the man, it would be credited with showing comparable intelligence to the human it had replaced. It is tempting to make a connection with Turing's enforced disguise of his own sexuality (Hodges 1983).

Aspects of the Turing test simultaneously reveal links to Turing's autobiography and to the cultural temper of the time. To reiterate, the period from the development of the telephone and the phonograph in the 1870s is sometimes characterized as one of secondary orality, in contradistinction to the primary orality of societies without written language. Secondary orality tends to be marked by an interest in, or allusions to and echoes of, primary orality (Ong 1982). The Turing test bears extensive similarities to a narrative developed in a primarily oral society – the Greek myth of Teiresias (*Encyclopaedia Britannica* 1911a).[1]

Teiresias was a Theban seer who was blind from his seventh year. Various causes for his blindness were alleged: one was that 'he had revealed to men what they ought not to know' (*Encyclopaedia Britannica* 1911a). Changes of sexuality are also involved. In one version of the story, Teiresias was originally a girl, but was changed into a boy by Apollo at the age of seven and then underwent several more transformations. An oracle was dedicated to Teiresias (*Encyclopaedia Britannica* 1911a; Graves 1955). It should be recalled that dialogue between questioner and responder at oracles allowed no direct sensory or visual contact between the questioner and responder and that the oracular voice might be disguised (Aune 1987; Bremmer 1987; Parke and Wormell 1956; Price 1985). The situation is therefore analogous to the removal from contact in the Turing test. For Homer, Teiresias was the only soul in Hades 'whose understanding even death has not impaired' (Homer 750 BCd: 168; Heubeck and Hoekstra 1989: 89). While losing all other human qualities in exile from the world of the living, intelligence alone is retained. In the Turing test, the man is replaced by a machine which, although similarly isolated from sensory and social contact, is required to keep the capacity for intelligent response.

Connections between the Turing test and twentieth-century logical and mathematical developments can be detected. In Turing's 1936 paper, it was shown that there could be no solution to the *Entscheidungsproblem* (see p. 69), as no general procedure for determining whether a particular Turing machine would ever halt when presented with a set of data could be established (Turing 1937). The halting problem for Turing machines seems to turn on the impossibility of finding a stable site outside an unbounded universe of discourse (Turing 1937). The Turing test reverses this process. First the man and then the computer are taken outside the universe of discourse, disguised or made unstable, and it is left to those within that universe of discourse to determine their identity.

Historically, the Turing test can be traced back to Descartes. In the *Discourse on Method*, Descartes speculated that physically convincing automata could not deceive us into believing that they were men, for 'they could never use words or other signs, composing them as we do to declare our thoughts to others'. A machine could be made to emit words, but not 'to arrange words in various ways to reply to the sense of everything that is said in its presence' (Descartes 1647: 73–4). For Descartes, the capacity for intelligent discourse was the faculty which distinguishes man from beasts and machines. An analogous distinction had been made by Aristotle: animals had voice but only man, as a political animal, had speech (Aristotle 323 BCc: 59–60). The Turing test follows Descartes in implicitly making the faculty for arranging signs the distinguishing human characteristic. However, it requires that an automaton be made which will attain the capacity for dialectic response denied to it by Descartes. The idea that intelligence can be sustained with limited sensory and social contact also reveals an acceptance of the Cartesian dichotomy between mind and body and of Descartes' emphasis on the asocial, rational individual as the source of certainty.

The attempt, in the subsequent development of models of human reasoning, to assimilate discourse about human affairs to a mathematical or logical model is comprehensible in its contemporary intellectual context. A.J. Ayer in *Language, Truth and Logic*, published in 1936 and subsequently influential, saw no difference in kind between the maxims of science and those of common sense (Ayer 1936: 65). In *The Mathematical Theory of Communication*, optimism was expressed that the model developed for the transmission of signals over telecommunication channels could be made to yield a sophisticated analysis of human communication: 'entropy not only speaks the language of arithmetic; it also speaks the language of language' (Shannon and Weaver 1949: 28). Subsequent research did not bear out this optimism (Fox 1983: 51–62). In linguistics, Chomsky's *Syntactic Structures*, published in 1957 and influenced by automata studies, regarded a human speaker as essentially an automaton (Chomsky 1957). Automata theory and formal logic are primarily concerned with the form of reasoning, not immediately with the interpretation of the primitive signs employed.

The idea that reasoning can be conducted without continuing reference to human interpretation of its content is also implicit in the idea of machine intelligence. An emphasis on the form, not the content, of arguments is present in Turing's intellectual context. In logic and mathematics, there had been a concern with the scope, and the limitations, of formal procedures not dependent on the meaning of the symbols manipulated (Boole 1854; Wittgenstein 1922; Church 1936; Post 1936; Turing 1937; Gandy 1988). For bibliography, W.W. Greg had prescribed that the bibliographer should be 'concerned with pieces of paper or parchment covered with certain written or printed signs . . . merely as arbitrary marks; their meaning is no business of his' (Greg 1932: 247). Shannon made an analogous methodological exclusion of the semantic aspects of communication from information theory in *The Mathematical Theory of Communication*, but used the term 'information' to refer to sequences of symbols (Shannon and Weaver 1949). A subtle criticism was later made of this choice of terms. The confusion generated between signals and information may not simply be a result of the misleading terminology. To some extent, at least, the confusion was the cause of the misleading terminology (Bar-Hillel 1955). In reducing information to signals, meaning is made an inherent property of messages and the human labour involved in their making and interpretation elided.

The emphasis of *Syntactic Structures* was on the form, not the content, of linguistic communication, although this contrast tends to be rendered as one between syntax and semantics (Chomsky 1957: 100–2). For Ryle in *The Concept of Mind*, which was published in 1949 and may have been a direct influence on Turing's 1950 paper (Hodges 1983: 418), the 'styles and procedures of people's activities *are* the way their minds work and not merely imperfect reflections of the postulated secret processes which were supposed to be the workings of minds' (Ryle 1949: 57). Two levels which can be distinguished for analytical purposes – those of expression and content – have been conflated with the expression given value in itself. An interest in the form, rather than with the content, of communication is, then, widely shared in Turing's intellectual context, although scarcely exclusive to it.

The shared emphasis on the form of communication, as well as the acceptance of the possibility of computer intelligence, can be partly explained by the bleakness of the Western political context of the early 1950s. The 1930s had witnessed the growth of Western intellectual optimism about the development of Soviet communism, and also the development of Fascism. Disillusion with Soviet communism had begun to grow with the news of the Moscow show trials of the late 1930s and with the Russo-German pact of 1941 (Warner 1983: 136–8). The collection of essays published in 1950, *The God that Failed*, which was concerned to 'study the state of mind of the Communist convert, and the atmosphere of the period – from 1917 to 1939 – when conversion was so common' (Crossman 1950: 7), testifies to the further loss of faith in this form of political progress. The Cold War began in the late 1940s (Hewison 1981: 24–33). The brutality of Nazism had been recognized but hardly understood. Later public comments on Nazism and Japanese militarism – for instance, those occasioned by Emperor Hirohito's visit to Britain in 1972 – tend to characterize Nazism as an aberration, a kind of unmotivated evil, whereas Japan's militarism is seen as closely connected with its culture. It is an attitude which preserves contemporary Europeans, and Americans, from implication in the guilt of either: if Nazism was seen as a product of German culture, then other Europeans would, to some extent, be implicated by the culture and humanity they share with Germany; and Japanese militarism is kept safely distant by being perceived as a culturally specific development (Warner 1984: 53–4). In the post-1945 political context, a stress on the form rather than the threatening and disturbing content of communication is comprehensible. The possibility of machine intelligence also promises a source of authority which would free a politically troubled culture from the responsibility for choice.

The external signs of intelligence, or intelligent behaviour, are implicitly equated with its inner presence by the development of the Turing test. Identifying intelligence with intelligent behaviour has been regarded as radically behaviourist (Harris 1987a: 27–35). Turing's own position is subtle, although it lends itself to ambiguous interpretation. In 'Computing machinery and intelligence', the question 'Can a machine display intelligent behaviour?' is advanced as an adequate, and clearer, substitute for the vague and difficult question 'Can a machine think?'. The subsequent development of speculations for computer intelligence, at least until Searle's intervention, tended to be less subtly qualified and to take the behavioural signs of intelligence as an unequivocal equivalent to intelligence (Searle 1980).

One effect of substituting considerations of intelligent behaviour for intelligence is partly to evade the difficult issue of what is meant by intelligence. In such circumstances, it is difficult to see why an obligation for definition should fall on critics, but some distinctions can be indicated. The Turing test implies, but does not state, that intelligence can be identified with the faculty for arranging signs and for producing written discourse. Even the name Teiresias can be rendered as 'he who delights in signs' (Graves 1955, volume 2: 409). From a semiotic perspective, intelligence and signification have been viewed as a single process (Eco 1976: 31). There is an unexpected concordance between the interpretation of human intelligence implied by the Turing test and one explicitly developed in semiotics.

The stress on the form of reasoning and the elements of behaviourism in the Turing test were seized upon by Searle in his refutation of its adequacy as an indicator of literal intelligence. Computational operations on purely formally defined elements had no necessary connection with understanding. In an analogous distinction, Searle described computers as operating syntactically without a semantic content. Understanding and semantic content were subsumed under the more technical term 'intentionality', the characteristic of mental states directed at objects or states of affairs in the world. For Searle, intentionality was essential to literal intelligence. Even an adequate simulation of intelligence would still lack this necessary quality (Searle 1980). Searle's refutation of the adequacy of the Turing test as an indicator of literal intelligence seems to have been widely accepted (Motzkin and Searle 1989).

The growth, and collapse, of speculations for the literal intelligence of computers can also be understood in relation to the concept of a paradigm – the constellation of beliefs and assumptions held in common by a scientific community – developed by Kuhn in *The Structure of Scientific Revolutions* (Kuhn 1962). Searle himself comments on the ideology of artificial intelligence. Its grip had made the implausible idea of literal computer intelligence plausible (Searle 1980). Speculations for computer intelligence had developed partly within specialized and, to some extent, enclosed research communities. Destructive intervention came from outside those research communities, from a perspective free from some of the characteristics of their paradigms.

Speculations for computer intelligence may also have been

stimulated, and partly protected, by the historical novelty of the technology. Other innovations in information technology have been associated with similar speculations. For instance, Lady Lovelace warned that Babbage's Analytical Engine had:

> no pretensions whatever to originate anything. It can do whatever we know how to order it to perform. It can follow analysis; but it has no power of anticipating any analytical relations or truths. Its province is to assist us in making available what we are already acquainted with.
>
> (Quoted in Bernstein 1965: 58)

Since 1950, and particularly since 1980, the date of Searle's intervention, computers have been increasingly incorporated into wider social life outside specialized research communities. Now that computers are familiar rather than mysterious objects, it is tempting to apply to claims for their literal intelligence a process of brutal persuasiveness analogous to Johnson's refutation of Berkeley's scepticism on the reality of the material world – 'I never shall forget the alacrity with which Johnson answered, striking his foot with mighty force against a large stone, till he rebounded from it "I refute it *thus*"' (Boswell 1791, volume 1: 471) – and to flick a switch without compunction, as we might close, although not burn, a book.

The discussion can now be summarized. In the tradition established by the Turing test, claims for the literal intelligence, or other cognitive state, of computers rested on the production of depersonalized linguistic responses to questions. Such claims foundered on the absence of intentionality, of a prior act of comprehension by the artefact. The growth, and collapse, of speculations for the literal intelligence of computers can be understood in terms of their intellectual and historical context, in relation to the continuing attempts to assimilate discourse about human affairs to a formal, logical model, and as a response to the bleakness of the post-1945 political context and to the novelty of the technology.

CONCLUSION

The perspective which links documents to computers through the presence of writing and through the human faculty for constructing systems of signs can then illuminate the issue of the literal intelligence of computers. Historical evidence supported a logically tenable position. Claims for the intelligence of computers and of documents in written language could be seen to rest on a similar basis: that depersonalized linguistic output was made available, usually at a distance in time and space from its original producer. Claims for the literal intelligence of computers and documents were subject to similar, although differently formulated, objections: that linguistic responses were made available without intentionality or understanding.

Scepticism about the value of a new information technology seems to be a sign of a movement towards intellectual maturity with regard to that technology. The measure of scepticism about the value of written language in the *Phaedrus* implies that its strangeness has been partly reduced by acquaintance and that it can be considered in relation to other forms of communication. Similarly, scepticism about the claims of computers to literal intelligence, and about the possibility of their being made to display intelligent behaviour, seems to indicate that they too have been partly assimilated into wider social life outside specialized research communities and can be rationally evaluated in relation to other methods for storing, manipulating and communicating information.

Reviewing claims for the intelligence of computers is itself part of this evaluative process. Several interconnected factors seemed to have motivated belief in the possibility of computer intelligence. The anxieties associated with the historical novelty of the information technology are one plausible motivation. The tradition of logical analysis associated, for instance, with Aristotle, Descartes, Leibniz and Boole, which attempted to reduce discourse about human affairs to a logical or mechanical model, emerged as a further influence. The emphasis on expression and formal modelling of human discourse in post-war linguistics and information theory could itself be seen as extension of this logical tradition. It could also be understood in relation to the political context. Following the political traumas of the 1930s and 1940s, there appeared to be an unconscious search for an account of meaning which would concentrate only on expression and avoid having to face its disturbing content; for a model of human consciousness which would refer choice to a formal system or automaton; and for an external, oracular authority which could take responsibility for political decisions. With the collapse of claims for the literal intelligence of an appropriately programmed computer, and the decline of optimism about attaining a convincing simulation of intelligence, we are returned to a soberer world. We can consult the products of the semiotic faculty, whether in computer or documentary form, and confer meaning on signs by interpreting them, but can no longer hope for objective instruction or advice from a site beyond humanity and dehumanized.

Chapter 6

Conclusion

But of such a diffused nature, and so large is the Empire of
Truth, that it hath place within the walls of Hell, and the Devils
themselves are daily forced to practise it . . . whether in the
conformity of words unto things, or things unto their own
conceptions, they practise truth in common among themselves. . . . although they deceive us, they lie not unto each
other; as well understanding that all community is continued
by Truth, and that of Hell cannot consist without it.

(Browne 1646: 76)

INTRODUCTION

Communicative practices which had tended to be regarded as
natural can be exposed as historically specific by transitions in
methods for communicating and storing information. They can
be questioned and their significance elucidated. For instance, it
was when oral communication and personal memory was being
extensively supplemented by the use of written language in Ancient
Greece that the informative role of poetry in primary orality was
strongly registered (Havelock 1982: 136). Similarly, when functions
once primarily associated with written language – transmission
of information over space and time – had also been assumed by
the audio and audio-visual media of secondary orality, it became
possible to begin to investigate the significance of writing and its
relation to speech. The development, in computer programming,
of a socially significant form of writing never intended as a communicative substitute for speech seems to have been a further
stimulus to investigation (Derrida 1976: 9; Harris 1986: 158).
Conversely, developments in information technology which are

initially regarded as strange and radically new can be placed in relation to pre-existing media as they are assimilated into wider social life.

This book has been concerned with relating the new to the more familiar, particularly with connecting computers to documents. Its aim has been to assimilate and place the new, and to make strange and re-examine the familiar – for instance, the received idea of writing as a representation of speech. In particular, the challenge posed by D.F. McKenzie of establishing a 'unifying, intellectual principle' which would connect computing and books (McKenzie 1986: 42–3) has been addressed. The discussion has been intended for citizens of political communities, inescapably implicated in such issues, for students of the disciplines invoked in the course of the discussion – for instance, of linguistics, semiotics and information science – and to those students as citizens. It seems appropriate now to review and summarize what has been established.

SUMMARY

Semiotics, which tended to be formally defined as the study of systems of signs, was introduced. It was valued for its insistence on a single faculty for constructing socially shared systems of signs and as a source of subtle and incisive distinctions between types of sign and between aspects of the sign. A more specific purpose was also intended: to establish a conjoint classification of written language and computer programs in terms of the distinction of signifier, sign and signified. The terminology associated with the description of computer operations, of symbol and token manipulation, and of information processing was seen to be related to the disciplinary contexts – those of symbolic and mathematical logic and information theory – from which computing emerged. There could be confusion between the precise, technical senses prescribed for these terms in disciplinary discourse and the wider range of meanings they could obtain in ordinary discourse, where, for instance, information might be associated with meaning. From a semiotic perspective, both written language and computer programs could be comprehended within the analytical category of the signifier. It was suggested that this classification was valuable both for its incisive distinction between aspects of the sign, particularly the contrast with the signified, and for the common categorization of written language with computer programs and data.

The similarities implied between written language and computer programs by their comprehension within the category of the signifier could be made more specific by turning to the study of writing. A discussion of writing, and its relation to speech, could be greatly assisted by distinguishing diachronic from synchronic perspectives, that is consideration of a system of signs over time from consideration at a period taken as a single point in time. Not all discussions of writing had been fully informed by this distinction.

Written language had been partially disentangled from speech. Classic discussion of language tended to regard written language as a secondary system of signs, parasitic on speech. More recent developments, partly aided by technological developments which enabled the recording and inspection of utterances, had indicated extensive lexical and structural contrasts between written and spoken language. Neither the word nor the sentence had been satisfactorily isolated as a feature of utterance alone. Written language once had a communicative possibility denied to speech, that is the transmission of messages to receivers distant in space and time without immediate reliance on the memory of a human intermediary. Audio and audio-visual technologies, beginning with the late nineteenth century inventions of the telephone and phonograph, had weakened this distinction by allowing spoken language to be transmitted over space and time. Other distinctions between written and spoken language were still tenable, although they had to be carefully qualified. Written language is primarily visible not audible, although speech could also be significantly graphic. Writing can be linked to speech by coded correlation, not resemblance. As a graphic form, written language has historical links and contemporary affinities with other codes of inscription without a simple correlate in utterance, such as musical and choreographic notation. Contrasts between written and spoken language seldom constituted absolute differences. Rather than insisting on spoken and written language as independent systems of signs, it emerged as more helpful to think of them as two contrasting ways of giving form to language.

Recognition of contrasts between written and spoken language, and of the affinities of written language with codes of inscription without a simple correlate in utterance, led to a subtle position which, however, continued to acknowledge links between written and spoken language. One form of writing, exemplified by alphabetic written language, drew on models in utterance, but a connection with speech need not be made necessary for the recognition of writing. The boundaries between forms of writing connected with speech and those independent of it were uncertain and mutable. Both spoken and written language could be enlarged. For instance, graphic signs conceivably independent of utterance, such as mathematical notations, could be given verbal and then oral substitutes for the purposes of discussion. There might be a loss of exactness or clarity if verbal or oral substitutes were considered without reference to their graphic correlates. Determining the extent to which a form of writing was linked to utterance could be crucially dependent on the context available for interpretation.

The transition from orality to literacy, in the sense of the supplementing of oral communication by writing with established correlates in utterance, formed a further focus for study. Anxieties connected with the introduction of writing to primarily oral societies could, in some narrative episodes, be associated with the power obtained by those able to interpret written messages. Alphabetic written language emerged, not as a radical novelty, but as a development from a rich variety of graphic signification, whose relation to utterance remained uncertain. Some forms of spoken discourse found in oral societies, such as oracular pronouncements, also anticipate features subsequently strongly associated with written language, for instance its impersonality and removal from direct semantic ratification. The cultural effects of the transition from orality to literacy were difficult to determine. Some negative consequences, such as the disabling of oral poets, could be identified. One positive effect, which appeared to be connected with the inability of written language to explain itself, was the development, particularly by Plato and Aristotle, of the analytic activities subsequently differentiated as formal logic and grammar.

The issue of the literal intelligence of documents and computers could also be illuminated from the perspective developed. Historical evidence from the transition from orality to literacy supported a logically tenable position. Logically, it could be insisted that, in the tradition following from the Turing test, claims for the literal intelligence of an appropriately programmed computer rested on a similar basis to claims which could be made for the intelligence of documents – the making available of de-personalized linguistic output. Such claims are subject to the identical objection that linguistic output is made available without a prior act of comprehension by the artefact. A complaint that written words can offer only the appearance of intelligence, without its substance, was found in the *Phaedrus*. In that dialogue, the mutual illumination which could be obtained by participants in oral dialectic was strongly preferred to the inability of written language to explain itself. Written language is indicted for offering the appearance of intelligence without its substance:

> written words . . . seem to talk to you as though they were intelligent, but if you question them anything about what they say, from a desire to be instructed, they go on telling you just the same thing for ever
>
> (Plato 400 BCa: 158)

This complaint had to be understood in its historical context of the supplementing of oral communication by written language. The meaning given to intelligence in the *Phaedrus* is difficult to elucidate fully, although it was connected with the ability to offer further clarification of statements. Similarly, the extent of comparability with modern ideas of intelligence, themselves multivalent and mutable over time, was difficult to determine.

On the interpretation of writing established, a computer program could be recognized as a written artefact which may have complex connections with written language. For instance, the design of programming languages seems to have been influenced, both deliberately and less consciously, by models available from familiar forms of writing, such as logical symbolisms and the written vernacular. For information-processing machines such as computers, ideas of energy and motion can be replaced by logical operations and logical events. In contrast to pre-existing written analogues to programs, the logical operations specified by a program could now be executed by a working computer rather than simply, if even, indicated.

An account of the primitive logical operations associated with the computer was required, for the sake of completeness. Automata theory offered models which allowed an enquirer to avoid real-world problems over the definition of a program – for instance, its distinction from a collection of data – and of a computer. The

development of automata theory had been publicly acknowledged to have been partly separate from the construction of
working computers. A comparative reading also suggested that it
had not been fully integrated with other aspects of formal and
mathematical logic. A consensus had emerged on the use of the
Turing machine model for use in exposition, although other formulations, such as those of Church and Post, were acknowledged
to be equivalent in computational power. A further aspect of the
consensus was that a process was computable if, and only if, it
was Turing-machine computable and that modifications to
Turing machines did not enlarge their computational power. In
order to deepen the understanding of the computational process,
deterministic Turing machines, applied to numerical and
taxonomic domains, were exemplified and a non-deterministic
Turing machine was recast as a deterministic Turing machine.
The universal Turing machine was introduced and defined as a
Turing machine which would precisely imitate the motions of
another Turing machine. The difficulty and elusiveness of the
concept of universality was only matched by its simplicity, once
grasped.

Semiotic aspects of the computational process were reviewed:
the construction of extensive computations seemed to become
dependent on the symbolism available and the exactness
obtainable from writing. In these respects, construction of
computational processes was analogous to the dependence on
notation for conceptual development alluded to in some discussions of mathematics. Formal logic was also advanced as an
example of a form of discourse critically dependent for its
development on graphic notation. Logic as a symbolic system
was distinguished from logic as the analysis of thought.

Connections between automata theory and formal logic were
further explored. It was suggested that the distinction between
the Turing machine model and the primitive formulations of
symbolic logic could be read, not as a dichotomy between an
absolute definition and a linguistically relative formulation, but
as a contrast between types of sign, along a continuum from the
iconic to the notational. An account of the object-language of
formal logic, associated with Wittgenstein and Ramsey, and analogous to the consensus of Turing machine theory, was thereby
rendered more persuasive. The Turing machine model could
then be read both as an account of the computational process,

which had not yet been falsified, and as analogous to the primitive formulations of symbolic logic.

Correlations from Turing machine theory to working computers were indicated. A Turing machine corresponded to a program; the symbols accepted on its tape to input data; the symbols written on the tape to output data or intermediate stages in computation; and the universal Turing machine to a computer. The computer itself could be regarded as a universal information machine which is transformed into the particular information machine specified by a program. It was concluded that the value of the Turing machine model lay in its widespread inter-subjectivity. It had given a model which had remained relatively stable over time and which had enabled those interested in the computational process to avoid difficulties arising from real-world complexity, such as the multiplicity of programming languages, the heterogeneity of programs, and historical changes in computer materials and architecture. One limitation of the inter-subjective scope of Turing machine theory was the tendency to give examples of procedures derived from mathematical or numerical domains which could obstruct access by other discursive communities interested in the computational process.

The historical and intellectual context for the development of claims for the intelligence of computers was reviewed. Several interconnected factors seem to have motivated belief in the possibility of computer intelligence: the apparent novelty of the technology; the continuing attempt to assimilate reasoning about human affairs to a mechanical or logical model; and the emphasis on expression, considered apart from content, and formal modelling of discourse in post-war linguistics and information theory. The bleakness of the post-war political context emerged as a further influence. A significant critique of claims for the literal intelligence of computers was made in 1980, at a point where computers were being increasingly assimilated into wider social life outside specialized research communities. The critique came from a research community different from those primarily associated with claims for computer intelligence. Analogies between the computer and the human brain or mind have tended to persist. The perspective established here, which articulates an analogy of computer programs with written language and other systems of signs, seems to be a further stage in assimilation in which the new is related to, and distinguished from, the more familiar.

Unifying principles for books and computers have, then, been established. Written language and computer programs are equally products of the semiotic faculty, for creating significant order. In particular, documents and computers are both unified, and differentiated, by the presence of writing. Written language is itself historically subsequent to speech as a product of the semiotic faculty, and computer programs can be regarded as a further development. The analogies between the computer and the human brain or mind, which have persisted since at least Turing's 1950 essay, 'Computing machinery and intelligence' (Turing 1950), have been displaced by a description based on writing and on the semiotic faculty, which promises to be of greater explanatory power.

CONCLUSION

A subtle, but still radical, change in perspective on a subject for study can expose science as myth. In this instance, the strong analogies between the computer and the human mind or brain have been revealed as a deceptive model whose development can be plausibly connected with the novelty of the technology and its intellectual and historical context. More gently, they could be seen as a special case of an encompassing paradigm, and do draw attention to the way in which communicative artefacts have served as models of consciousness, often in subdued and implicit rather than explicit analogies. Even in the *Phaedrus*, the permanency of writing is valued when it is appealed to as a model for knowledge integrated into personal consciousness: 'written on the soul of the hearer' (Plato 400 BCb: 101). More familiarly, in an analogy traceable to Aristotle, Locke compared the unformed mind to a 'white paper void of all characters, without any *ideas*' (Locke 1690, volume 1: 77). An implicit analogy is made between the mind and a communicative artefact in Milton's defence of the liberty of unlicensed printing: 'as good almost kill a Man as kill a good Book' (Milton 1644: 201). Communicative artefacts can serve as models for consciousness and, through interaction with their interpreters, change consciousness, although in subtle and possibly elusive ways.

Scepticism towards claims made for the value of an information technology was earlier advanced as a sign of a movement towards intellectual maturity with regard to that technology. Signs of such a sceptical reaction, and then of considered evaluation, are begun to emerge. Apocalyptic prophecies of a transition to an information society, emblematized by the computer (Bell 1980: 509), have been supplemented by cautious reservations that 'detailed empirical studies . . . suggest that there is no automatic effect from the technology itself' (Finnegan 1989: 117). Other discussions have also conceded that it is difficult to isolate those social and cultural changes which can be causally connected with changes in information technology, either in historical study or for prediction (Morpurgo Davies 1986: 69). Where the effects of the introduction of new information technologies can be isolated, at least for analytical purposes, information appears to be a dependent rather than a primary variable. For instance, the 'recent introduction of printing into non-literate societies has seldom endorsed our traditional view of its efficacy as an agent of change' (McKenzie 1986: 52). Scepticism carries destructive dangers of its own, but, followed by detailed analysis, it can create room for considered evaluation of claims made for computers and their effects on societies.

A positive proposition can be developed from the recognition of writing and the faculty for constructing systems of signs as uniting, and differentiating, documents and computers. Spoken language can be regarded as one social sign-system among others, such as written language, other forms of writing, codes of gesture, symbolic rites and the like. To repeat Saussure, in his brief although highly significant exception to the explicit attention of linguistics to spoken language: 'it is not spoken language which is natural to man, but the faculty of constructing a language, i.e. a system of distinct signs corresponding to distinct ideas' (Saussure 1916: 10). Linguistics has reiterated the proposition that there are no primitive spoken languages, in that all discovered cultures have developed languages sufficient to meet their communicational needs. Recognition of spoken language as one among other social sign-systems, and of a single faculty for constructing such systems, seems to legitimate an extension of this proposition to include other sign-systems, including writing: that, subject to delays, societies develop methods for storing and communicating information sufficient to meet their needs. It seems appropriate to conclude with a similar point from a written, and published, report of an otherwise transitory utterance: 'Society is held together by communication and information. . . . Do the devils lie? No; for then Hell could not subsist' (Boswell 1791: volume 3: 293).

Notes

1 SEMIOTICS

1 Differences can be discovered between semiotics and semiology: for instance, semiotics may seek antecedents in philosophical texts while semiology may prefer linguistics. Such differences are contrasting tendencies not clear mutual demarcations. Texts in the English language tend to prefer 'semiotics' and this convention will be followed here.

4 COMPUTERS

1 The literature of automata studies is profuse. I have deliberately restricted references to those texts taken to be particularly significant. A similar restraint has been observed with regard to the literature of formal logic.

2 The discussion here implies that an unrestricted number of machine states and an unlimited symbol space are sufficient for both growing and infinite automata. This is intended as an acceptable simplification of a complex issue which would seem to have a parallel in debates within philosophy and mathematics on whether infinity is substantively different from number. The position implicitly endorsed here is that indicated by Vico (1710), that human constructions can be only nominally infinite:

> the truth is that those genera are only nominally infinite, since man is neither nothing nor everything. Consequently, he cannot think about nothing, except by the negation of something; nor can he think about the infinite except by the negation of the finite . . . .
> these sciences create the truths they teach. Man contains within himself a fictitious world of lines and numbers, and he operates in it with his abstractions just as God operates with reality.
>
> (Vico 1710: 63, 123)

3 A distinction between non-deterministic and probabilistic automata is also made (Minsky 1967: 15).

4 This observation is based on experience of translating from written Old English and Japanese to modern English prose, using a grammar and a dictionary.

5 The logical expression and its diagrammatic correlate are freely adapted from the definition. They deliberately embody the view of negation derivable from the *Tractatus Logico-philosophicus* (Wittgenstein 1922) in which the negative of a term is not identified with any positive quality. Only that node of the binary tree which corresponds to the logical statement has been labelled. Labels could be given to other nodes.

5 INTELLIGENCE OF COMPUTERS

1 Artificial intelligence has subsequently shown elements of secondary orality, for instance in the practice of knowledge elicitation from experts and in its fondness for oracular names for projects. Teiresias would be more familiarly known as an expert system for diagnosing blood infections (Aleksander 1984: 132).

Recommended reading

INTRODUCTION

For an enunciation of the issues which this book attempts to develop:
D.F. McKenzie, *Bibliography and the Sociology of Texts* (The Panizzi Lectures 1985), London, British Library, 1986.

1 SEMIOTICS

The following texts are of particular significance for the topics covered, or alluded to, in this chapter.

Semiotics

F. de Saussure, *Course in General Linguistics*, edited by C. Bally and A. Sechehaye with the collaboration of A. Riedlinger, first published 1916, translated and annotated by R. Harris, London, Duckworth, 1983. Particularly pp. 10–17.

R. Barthes, 'Elements of semiology', in R. Barthes, *Writing Degree Zero & Elements of Semiology*, translated from the French by A. Lavers and C. Smith, London, Jonathan Cape, 1984.

Semiotics and information studies

For an application of semiotic distinctions to indexing languages, while making reservations on the scope of semiotics:
J.-C. Gardin, 'Document analysis and linguistic theory', *Journal of Documentation*, 29, 2, 1973: 137–68.

For a discussion of the relation between information science and semiotics:
J. Warner, 'Semiotics, information science, documents and computers', *Journal of Documentation*, 46, 1, 1990: 16–32.

For systematic distinctions between levels of discourse concerning information technology:

J. Liebenau and J. Backhouse, *Understanding Information: An Introduction*, Houndsmill, Macmillan Education, 1990.

2 WRITING

The following texts are of particular significance for the topics covered, or alluded to, in this chapter.

For a valuable discussion of the difficulties of defining writing and isolating its effects on consciousness:

A. Morpurgo Davies, 'Forms of writing in the ancient Mediterranean world', in G. Baumann (ed.), *The Written Word: Literacy in Transition* (Wolfson College Lectures 1985), Clarendon Press, Oxford, 1986.

The following two texts are valuable for their wealth of detail and illustrations. Diringer's historical account is distorted by an alphabetical teleology, whereas Gaur regards all writing as of equal value.

D. Diringer, *The Alphabet: A Key to the History of Mankind*, 2 volumes, 3rd edition revised with the collaboration of R. Regensburger, London, Hutchison, 1968.

A. Gaur, *A History of Writing*, revised edition, London, British Library, 1992.

For an early, although still significant, discussion of the transition from oral to oral and written linguistic communication:

J. Goody and I. Watt, 'The consequences of literacy', in J. Goody (ed.), *Literacy in Traditional Societies*, Cambridge, Cambridge University Press, 1968. First published in *Comparative Studies in Society and History*, 5, 1963: 304–45.

For the most sophisticated, although difficult, account of the development of alphabetic written language from pre-existing forms of writing:

R. Harris, *The Origin of Writing*, London, Duckworth, 1986.

For a significant challenge to the primacy of speech, which has provoked much subsequent response:

J. Derrida, *Of Grammatology*, translated by Gayatri Chakravorty Spivak, Baltimore and London, Johns Hopkins University Press, 1976.

For a fictional account of nineteenth-century deciphering of ancient scripts, more sympathetic and revealing than the science it parodies:

Mark Twain, 'Some learned fables for good old boys and girls', in C. Neider (ed.), *The Complete Short Stories of Mark Twain*, New York, Bantam Books, 1981. First published 1875.

For a detailed study of the interpretation accorded to writing for the purposes of claims to intellectual property in the United Kingdom and the United States:

J. Warner, 'Writing and literary work in copyright: a binational and historical analysis', *Journal of the American Society for Information Science*, 44, 6, 1993: 307–21.

3 INTELLIGENCE OF DOCUMENTS

Two modern translations of the *Phaedrus* are relatively easily obtainable:
Plato, *Phaedrus and the Seventh and Eighth Letters*, translated with an
 introduction by Walter Hamilton, Harmondsworth, Penguin, 1973.
Plato, *Plato's Phaedrus*, translated with an introduction and commentary
 by R. Hackforth, Cambridge, Cambridge University Press, 1952.

For an account of the influence of written language on the development
of formal logic and grammar:
R. Harris, 'How does writing restructure thought?', *Language and Communication*, 9, 2/3, 1989: 99–106.

4 COMPUTERS

For one aspect of the complex prehistory of working automata:
M. Gardner, *Logic Machines and Diagrams*, first published 1958, 2nd edition,
 Brighton, Harvester, 1983.

For a collection of significant source documents in the development of
mathematical logic and automata theory:
M. Davis (ed.), *The Undecidable: Basic Papers on Undecidable Propositions,
 Unsolvable Problems and Computable Functions*, Hewlett, NY, Raven
 Press, 1965.

For a recent historical perspective on the development of Turing machine
theory:
R. Herken, *The Universal Turing Machine: A Half-Century Survey*, Oxford,
 Oxford University Press, 1988.

For a comprehensive study of automata and mathematical logic, from
which the notation used in this chapter was derived:
G.S. Boolos and R.C. Jeffrey, *Computability and Logic*, first published 1974,
 3rd edition, Cambridge, Cambridge University Press, 1989.

For a treatment of automata theory which gives a clear account of different
formulations for the universal Turing machine:
M. L. Minsky, *Computation: Finite and Infinite Machines*. Englewood Cliffs,
 NJ, Prentice-Hall, 1967.

5 INTELLIGENCE OF COMPUTERS

The following texts are of particular significance for the topics covered,
or alluded to, in this chapter:
A.M. Turing, 'Computing machinery and intelligence', in A.R. Anderson,
 (ed.), *Minds and Machines*, Englewood Cliffs, NJ, Prentice-Hall, 1964.
 First published 1950. Also reprinted in various other collections.
J.R. Searle, 'Minds, brains and programs', *The Behavioral and Brain Sciences*, 3,
 1980: 417–57.

Bibliography

Ackrill, J.L. (1963) 'Notes', in *Aristotle's Categories and De Interpretatione*, trans. J.L. Ackrill 1989, Oxford: Clarendon Press.

Aleksander, I. (1984) *Designing Intelligent Systems: An Introduction*, London: Kogan Page.

Aleksander, I. and Burnett, P. (1987) *Thinking Machines: The Search for Artificial Intelligence*, Oxford: Oxford University Press.

Alston, R. (1988) 'Review of B.H. Rudall and T.N. Corns, *Computers and Literature*', *Library*, 10, 2: 173–6.

Aristotle. (323 BCa) 'Categories', in *Aristotle's Categories and De Interpretatione*, trans. J.L. Ackrill 1989, Oxford: Clarendon Press.

—— (323 BCb) 'De interpretatione', in *Aristotle's Categories and De Interpretatione*, trans. J.L. Ackrill 1989, Oxford: Clarendon Press.

—— (323 BCc) *The Politics*, trans. T.A. Sinclair, revised and re-presented T.J. Saunders 1981, Harmondsworth: Penguin.

Augustine (398) *Confessions*, 1961, trans. and intr. R.S. Pine-Coffin, London: Penguin.

Aune, D.E. (1987) 'Oracles', in E. Mircea (ed.), *The Encyclopaedia of Religion*, New York: Macmillan, and London: Collier-Macmillan, 2: 80–7.

Ayer, A.J. (1936) *Language, Truth and Logic*, 1971, Harmondsworth: Penguin.

Bacon, F. (1597) 'Of studies', in *The Essays*, ed. and intr. J. Pitcher 1985, Harmondsworth, Middlesex and New York: Penguin.

Bar-Hillel, Y. (1955) 'An examination of information theory', in Y. Bar-Hillel, *Language and Information: Selected Essays on their Theory and Application*, 1964, Reading, MA: Addison-Wesley, and Jerusalem: Jerusalem Academic Press.

Barthes, R. (1973) *Mythologies*, selected and trans. A. Lavers, London: Collins.

—— (1982) 'The photographic message', in S. Sontag (ed.), *A Barthes Reader*, London: Jonathan Cape.

—— (1984) 'Elements of semiology', in R. Barthes, *Writing Degree Zero & Elements of Semiology*, trans. A. Lavers and C. Smith, London: Jonathan Cape.

Baumann, G. (1986) *The Written Word: Literacy in Transition* (Wolfson College Lectures 1985), Oxford: Clarendon Press.

Bavel, Z. (1987) *Introduction to the Theory of Automata*, Reston, VA: Reston Publishing Company.

B.D.J. (1911) 'Linnaeus', in *Encyclopaedia Britannica*, 11th edn, Cambridge: Cambridge University Press, 16: 732–3.

Bell, D. (1980) 'The social framework of the information society', in T. Forester (ed.), *The Microelectronics Revolution: The Complete Guide to the New Technology and its Impact on Society*, Oxford: Basil Blackwell.

Bell, E.T. (1937) *Men of Mathematics*, 2 volumes, London: Penguin.

Bentham, J. (1780) *An Introduction to the Principles of Morals and Legislation*, 1907, Oxford: Clarendon Press.

Berger, P.L. and Luckmann, T. (1966) *The Social Construction of Reality*, 1985, Harmondsworth: Penguin.

Berlin, I. (1950) 'Logical translation', in I. Berlin, *Concepts and Categories: Philosophical Essays*, 1980, Oxford: Oxford University Press.

Bernstein, J. (1965) *The Analytical Engine: Computers – Past, Present and Future*, London: Secker & Warburg.

Biber, D. (1988) *Variation across Speech and Writing*, Cambridge: Cambridge University Press.

Bochenski, I.M. (1961) *History of Formal Logic*, trans. I. Thomas, Indiana: University of Notre Dame Press.

Bolter, J.D. (1984) *Turing's Man: Western Culture in the Computer Age*, Chapel Hill: University of North Carolina Press.

Boole, G. (1854) *An Investigation of the Laws of Thought, on which are Founded the Mathematical Theories of Logic and Probabilities*, London: Walton and Maberly, and Cambridge: Macmillan.

Boolos, G.S. and Jeffrey, R.C. (1974) *Computability and Logic*, 3rd edn 1989, Cambridge: Cambridge University Press.

Boswell, J. (1791) *Boswell's Life of Johnson*, 6 volumes, ed. G.B. Hill, revised and enlarged edn L.F. Powell 1934, Oxford: Clarendon Press.

Bremmer, J. (1987) 'Delphi', in E. Mircea (ed.), *The Encyclopaedia of Religion*, New York: Macmillan, and London: Collier-Macmillan, 4: 277–9.

Brody, B.A. (1967) 'Logical terms, glossary of', in P. Edwards (ed.), *The Encyclopaedia of Philosophy*, New York: Macmillan, and London: The Free Press, 5: 57–77.

Browne, T. (1646) *Pseudoxia Epidemica*, in G. Keynes (ed.), *The Works of Sir Thomas Browne*, 1965, London: Faber & Faber.

Burn, A.R. (1972) 'Introduction', in Herodotus, *The Histories*, 1972, trans. A. de Selincourt and revised A.R. Burn, London: Penguin.

Chapman, R. (1984) *The Treatment of Sounds in Language and Literature*, Oxford and London: Basil Blackwell in association with Andre Deutsch.

Charniak, E. and McDermott, D. (1985) *Introduction to Artificial Intelligence*, Reading, MA: Addison-Wesley.

Cherry, C. (1957) *On Human Communication: Review, a Survey and a Criticism*, 3rd edn 1978, Cambridge, MA, and London: MIT Press.

Chomsky, N. (1957) *Syntactic Structures*, The Hague: Mouton.

Church, A. (1936) 'An unsolvable problem of elementary number theory', in M. Davis (ed.), *The Undecidable: Basic Papers on Undecidable Propositions, Unsolvable Problems and Computable Functions*, 1965, Hewlett, NY: Raven Press.

Churchland, P.M. and Churchland, P.D. (1990) 'Could a machine think?', *Scientific American*, 262, 1: 26–31.

Copi, I.M. (1953) *Introduction to Logic*, 6th edn 1982, New York: Macmillan, and London: Collier-Macmillan.

Copyright and Designs (1977) *Copyright and Designs Law: Report of the Committee to Consider the Laws on Copyright and Designs, Chairman the Honourable Mr Justice Whitford* (Cmnd 6732), London: Her Majesty's Stationery Office.

Crawley, E. (1931) *Dress, Drinks, and Drums: Further Studies of Savages and Sex*, London: Methuen.

Crossman, R. (1950) *The God that Failed: Six Studies in Communism*, London: Hamish Hamilton.

Crystal, D. (1985) *Linguistics*, 2nd edn, Harmondsworth: Penguin.

—— (1987) *The Cambridge Encyclopaedia of Language*, Cambridge: Cambridge University Press.

Culler, J. (1976) *Saussure*, 6th impression with revisions 1988, London: Fontana.

Darwin, C. (1859) *The Origin of Species by Means of Natural Selection or The Preservation of Favoured Races in the Struggle for Life*, ed. J.W. Burrow 1968, London: Penguin.

Data Protection Act. (1984) Data Protection Act 1984. An Act to regulate the use of automatically processed information relating to individuals and the provision of services in respect of such information. 1984 c.35.

Davies, M. (1987) 'Reading cases', *The Modern Law Review*, 50, 4: 409–31.

Davis, M. (1956) 'A note on universal Turing machines', in C.E. Shannon and J. McCarthy (eds), *Automata Studies*, 1956, Princeton, NJ: Princeton University Press.

—— (1958) *Computability and Unsolvability*, 1982, New York: Dover Publications.

—— (1965) *The Undecidable: Basic Papers on Undecidable Propositions, Unsolvable Problems and Computable Functions*. Hewlett, NY: Raven Press.

—— (1988a) 'Mathematical logic and the origin of modern computing', in R. Herken (ed.), *The Universal Turing Machine: A Half-century Survey*, Oxford: Oxford University Press.

—— (1988b) 'Influences of mathematical logic on computer science', in R. Herken (ed.), *The Universal Turing Machine: A Half-century Survey*, Oxford: Oxford University Press.

Delong, H. (1970) *A Profile of Mathematical Logic*, Reading, MA: Addison-Wesley.

Derrida, J. (1976) *Of Grammatology*, trans. Gayatri Chakravorty Spivak, Baltimore and London: Johns Hopkins University Press.

Descartes, R. (1647) *Discourse on Method and the Meditations*, trans. F.E. Sutcliffe 1968, London: Penguin.

Dickens, C. (1854) *Hard Times*, 1989, Oxford and New York: Oxford University Press.

—— (1861) *Great Expectations*, 1991, London: Mandarin.

Dijkstra, E.W. (1989) 'On the cruelty of really teaching computer science' (The SIGCSE Award Lecture 1989), *SIGCSE Bulletin: A*

Quarterly Publication of the Special Interest Group on Computer Science Education, 21, 1: xxiv–xxxix.

Diringer, D. (1968) *The Alphabet: A Key to the History of Mankind*, 2 volumes, 3rd edn revised with the collaboration of R. Regensburger, London: Hutchison.

Donovan, E. (1820) *The Natural History of British Quadrapeds; Consisting of Coloured Figures, Accompanied with Scientific and General Descriptions, of All the Species that are Known to Inhabit the British Isles . . . and also such . . .*, London: Printed for the Author, and for F.C. and J. Rivington.

Eco, U. (1976) *A Theory of Semiotics*, London and Bloomington: Indiana University Press.

—— (1984) *Semiotics and the Philosophy of Language*, London: Macmillan.

Edwards, M.W. (1992) *The Iliad: A Commentary*. Volume V: books 17–20. Cambridge: Cambridge University Press.

Egil (1230) *Egil's Saga*, 1976, trans. and intr. H. Pálsson and P. Edwards, Harmondsworth: Penguin.

Encyclopaedia Britannica (1910) 'Dualla', in *Encyclopaedia Britannica*, 11th edn, Cambridge: Cambridge University Press, 8: 614.

—— (1911a) 'Teiresias', in *Encyclopaedia Britannica*, 11th edn, Cambridge: Cambridge University Press, 26: 508.

—— (1911b) 'Writing', in *Encyclopaedia Britannica*, 11th edn, Cambridge: Cambridge University Press, 28: 852–3.

—— (1985) 'Writing', in *The New Encyclopaedia Britannica*, 15th edn, Chicago: Encyclopaedia Britannica, 29: 982–1035.

Fauvel, M. and Gray, J. (1987) *The History of Mathematics: A Reader*, Houndsmill, Basingstoke and Milton Keynes: Macmillan Press in association with the Open University.

Febvre, L. and Martin, H.-J. (1976) *The Coming of the Book: The Impact of Printing 1450–1800*, trans. D. Gerard and ed. G. Nowell-Smith and D. Wootton, London: New Left Books.

Finnegan, R. (1970) *Oral Literature in Africa*, Oxford: Clarendon Press.

—— (1989) 'Communication and technology', *Language and Communication: An Interdisciplinary Journal*, 9: 107–27.

Fleck, L. (1935) *Genesis and Development of a Scientific Fact*, trans. F. Bradley and T.J. Treen and ed. T.J. Trenn and R.K. Merton 1979, Chicago: Chicago University Press.

Ford, N. (1989) 'From information- to knowledge-management: the role of rule induction and neural net machine learning techniques in knowledge generation', *Journal of Information Science*, 15: 299–304.

Fox, C.J. (1983) *Information and Misinformation: An Investigation of the Notions of Information, Misinformation, Informing and Misinforming*, London and Westport: Greenwood Press.

Galeano, E. (1987) *Genesis*, trans. C. Belfrage, London: Methuen.

Gandy, R. (1988) 'The confluence of ideas in 1936', in R. Herken (ed.), *The Universal Turing Machine: A Half-century Survey*, Oxford: Oxford University Press.

Gardin, J.-C. (1973) 'Document analysis and linguistic theory', *Journal of Documentation*, 29, 2: 137–68.

Gardner, M. (1958) *Logic Machines and Diagrams*, 2nd edn 1983, Brighton: Harvester.

Gaur, A. (1984) *A History of Writing*, revised edn 1992, London: British Library.

Gissing, G. (1891) *New Grub Street*, London: Smith, Elder.

Gödel, K. (1946) 'Remarks before the Princeton bicentennial conference on problems in mathematics', in M. Davis (ed.), *The Undecidable: Basic Papers on Undecidable Propositions, Unsolvable Problems and Computable Functions*, 1965, Hewlett, NY: Raven Press.

Goody, J. (1968) 'Introduction', in J. Goody (ed.), *Literacy in Traditional Societies*, Cambridge: Cambridge University Press.

—— (1977) *The Domestication of the Savage Mind*, Cambridge: Cambridge University Press.

Goody, J. and Watt, I. (1963) 'The consequences of literacy', in J. Goody (ed.), *Literacy in Traditional Societies*, 1968, Cambridge: Cambridge University Press.

Graves, R. (1955) *The Greek Myths*, 2 volumes, 1960, London: Penguin.

Greg, W.W. (1932) 'Bibliography – an apologia', in W.W. Greg, *Collected Papers*, 1966, ed. J.C. Maxwell, Oxford: Clarendon Press.

Guest, A.H. (1985) 'Dance, The art of', in *The New Encyclopaedia Britannica*, 15th edn, Chicago: Encyclopaedia Britannica, 16: 986–1008.

Hamilton, W. (1973) 'Introduction', in Plato, *Phaedrus and the Seventh and Eighth Letters*, trans. and intr. W. Hamilton, Harmondsworth: Penguin.

Harris, R. (1980) *The Language-makers*, London: Duckworth.

—— (1986) *The Origin of Writing*, London, Duckworth.

—— (1987a) *The Language Machine*, London: Duckworth.

—— (1987b) *Reading Saussure: A Critical Commentary on the Cours de Linguistique Generale*, London: Duckworth.

—— (1989) 'How does writing restructure thought?', *Language and Communication*, 9, 2/3: 99–106.

Hartley, J. (1982) *Understanding News*, London: Methuen.

Havelock, E.A. (1982) *The Literate Revolution in Greece and its Cultural Consequences*, Princeton, NJ: Princeton University Press.

Herken, R. (1988) *The Universal Turing Machine: A Half-Century Survey*, Oxford: Oxford University Press.

Herodotus (430 BC) *The Histories*, 1972, trans. A. de Selincourt and revised A.R. Burn, London: Penguin.

Heubeck, A. and Hoekstra, A. (1989) *A Commentary on Homer's Odyssey*. Volume II: books 9–16. Oxford: Clarendon Press.

Heubeck, A., West, S. and Hainsworth, J.B. (1988) *A Commentary on Homer's Odyssey*. Volume I: Introduction and books 1–8. Oxford: Clarendon Press.

Hewison, R. (1981) *In Anger: British Culture in the Cold War 1945–60*, 2nd edn, London: Methuen.

Hodges, A. (1983) *Alan Turing: The Enigma*, London: Burnett Books in association with Hutchison Publishing Group.

Hodges, W. (1977) *Logic*, Harmondsworth: Penguin.

Homer (750 BCa) *The Iliad*, trans. R. Fitzgerald and intr. G.S. Kirk, 1984, Oxford: Oxford University Press.

Homer (750 BCb) *The Iliad*, trans. and intr. M. Hammond, 1987, London, Penguin.

—— (750 BCc) *The Iliad*, trans. R. Fagles and intr. B. Knox, 1991, New York, Penguin.

—— (750 BCd) *The Odyssey*, 1946, trans. E.V. Rieu, Harmondsworth: Penguin.

—— (750 BCe) *The Odyssey*, 1975, trans. and intr. Richard Lattimore. New York: Harper & Row.

—— (750 BCf) *The Odyssey*, 1980, trans. Walter Shewring and intr. G.S. Kirk, Oxford: Oxford University Press.

Illich, I. and Sanders, B (1988) *ABC: The Alphabetization of the Popular Mind*, 1989, New York: Vintage Books.

Janko, R. (1992) *The Iliad: A Commentary*. Volume IV: books 13–16. Cambridge: Cambridge University Press.

Johnson, S. (1755a) *A Dictionary of the English Language*, 1818, London: Longman.

—— (1775b) 'Preface to the Dictionary', in E.L. McAdam and G. Milne, *Johnson's Dictionary: A Modern Selection*, 1982, London and Basingstoke: Macmillan.

Johnson-Laird, P.N. (1988) *The Computer and the Mind: an Introduction to Cognitive Science*, London: Fontana.

Kirk, G.S. (1985) *The Iliad: A Commentary*. Volume I: books 1–4. Cambridge: Cambridge University Press.

—— (1990) *The Iliad: A Commentary*. Volume II: books 5–8. Cambridge: Cambridge University Press.

Kleene, S.C. (1936) 'General recursive functions of natural numbers' (Presented to the American Mathematical Society September 1935), in M. Davis (ed.), *The Undecidable: Basic Papers on Undecidable Propositions, Unsolvable Problems and Computable Functions*, 1965, Hewlett, NY: Raven Press.

Kneale, W.K. and Kneale, M. (1962) *The Development of Logic*, Oxford: Clarendon Press.

Knowles, F. (1987) 'Margaret Masterman: her life and work (an appreciation by an erstwhile colleague)', in K.P. Jones (ed.), *Meaning: The Frontier of Informatics* (Informatics 9: Proceedings of a conference jointly sponsored by Aslib, the Aslib Informatics Group, and the Information Retrieval Specialist Group of the British Computer Society, King's College, Cambridge, 26–27 March 1987), London: Aslib.

Kuhn, T.S. (1962) *The Structure of Scientific Revolutions*, 2nd edn 1970, Chicago and London: University of Chicago Press.

Laver, M. (1983) *Information, Technology and Libraries* (The First British Library Annual Research Lecture), London: British Library.

Leibniz, G.W. (1686) 'Primary truths', in G.W. Leibniz, *Philosophical Writings*, ed. G.H.R. Parkinson and trans. M. Morris and G.H.R. Parkinson 1973, London: J.M. Dent.

—— (1689) 'On freedom', in G.W. Leibniz, *Philosophical Writings* ed. G.H.R. Parkinson and trans. M. Morris and G.H.R. Parkinson 1973, London: J.M. Dent.

—— (1716) 'Correspondence with Clarke (selections)', in G.W. Leibniz,

Philosophical Writings, ed. G.H.R. Parkinson and trans. M. Morris and G.H.R. Parkinson 1973, London: J.M. Dent.

Leith, P. (1986a) 'Fundamental errors in legal logic programming', *The Computer Journal,* 29: 545–52.

―― (1986b) 'Legal expert systems: misunderstanding the legal process', *Computers and Law,* 49: 26–31.

―― (1990) *Formalism in AI and Computer Science,* New York: Ellis Horwood.

Lemmon, E.J. (1965) *Beginning Logic,* London: Nelson.

Liebenau, J. and Backhouse, J. (1990) *Understanding Information: An Introduction,* Houndsmill: Macmillan.

Linne, C. (1792) *The Animal Kingdom, or Zoological System, of the Celebrated Sir Charles Linnaeus. Class I. Mammalia: Containing a Complete Systematic Description, Arrangement, and Nomenclature, of all the Known Species and Varieties . . .,* Edinburgh: Printed for A. Strahan, T. Cadell.

Locke, J. (1690) *An Essay Concerning Human Understanding,* 2 volumes, 1965, London: Dent, and New York: Dutton.

Lord, A.B. (1960) *The Singer of Tales,* Cambridge, MA: Harvard University Press, and London: Oxford University Press.

Lyons, J. (1970) *Chomsky,* London: Fontana.

McArthur, T. (1986) *Worlds of Reference: Lexicography, Learning and Language from the Clay Tablet to the Computer,* 1988, Cambridge: Cambridge University Press.

McKenzie, D.F. (1986) *Bibliography and the Sociology of Texts* (The Panizzi Lectures 1985), London: British Library.

McKitterick, R. (1989) *The Carolingians and the Written Word,* Cambridge: Cambridge University Press.

Marschak, A. (1972) *The Roots of Civilization: The Cognitive Beginnings of Man's First Art, Symbol and Notation,* London: Weidenfeld and Nicolson.

Michie, D. (1988) 'The fifth generation's unbridged gap', in R. Herken (ed.), *The Universal Turing Machine: A Half-century Survey,* Oxford: Oxford University Press.

Mill, J.S. (1843) *A System of Logic Ratiocinative and Inductive: Being a Connected View of the Principles of Evidence and the Methods of Scientific Investigation,* ed. J.M. Robson and intr. R.F. McRae, in J.M. Robson (ed.), *Collected Works of John Stuart Mill,* 1973–1974, Toronto: University of Toronto Press, and London: Routledge and Kegan Paul.

―― (1873) *Autobiography,* ed. J. Stillinger 1971, Oxford: Oxford University Press.

Milton, J. (1644) *Aeropagitica,* in C.A. Patrides (ed.), *John Milton: Selected Prose,* revised edn 1985, Columbia: University of Missouri Press.

Minsky, M.L. (1967) *Computation: Finite and Infinite Machines,* Englewood Cliffs, NJ: Prentice-Hall.

Morpurgo Davies, A. (1986) 'Forms of writing in the ancient Mediterranean world', in G. Baumann (ed.), *The Written Word: Literacy in Transition* (Wolfson College Lectures 1985), Oxford: Clarendon Press.

Motzkin, E. and Searle, J.R. (1989) 'Artificial intelligence and the Chinese room: an exchange', *The New York Review of Books,* 16 February 1989: 44–5.

Newton-Smith, W.H. (1985) *Logic: An Introductory Course,* London: Routledge and Kegan Paul.

Njal (1280) *Njal's Saga*, 1960, trans. and intr. M. Magnusson and H. Pálsson, Harmondsworth: Penguin.

OED (1989) *The Oxford English Dictionary*, 2nd edn prepared by J.A. Simpson and E.S.C. Weiner 1989, Oxford: Clarendon Press.

Ollé, J.G. (1973) *An Introduction to British Government Publications*, London: Association of Assistant Librarians.

Ong, W.J. (1982) *Orality and Literacy: The Technologizing of the Word*, London and New York: Methuen.

—— (1986) 'Writing is a technology that restructures thought', in G. Baumann (ed.), *The Written Word: Literacy in Transition* (Wolfson College Lectures 1985), Oxford: Clarendon Press.

Page, N. (1973) *Speech in the English Novel*, London: Longman.

Parke, H.W. and Wormell, D.E.W. (1956) *The Delphic Oracle*. Volume I: The History. Volume II: The Oracular Responses. Oxford: Basil Blackwell.

Penrose, R. (1989) *The Emperor's New Mind: Concerning Computers, Minds, and the Laws of Physics*, Oxford: Oxford University Press.

Plato. (400 BCa) *Plato's Phaedrus*, trans. and intr. R. Hackforth 1952, Cambridge: Cambridge University Press.

—— (400 BCb) *Phaedrus*, in *Phaedrus and the Seventh and Eighth Letters*, trans. and intr. W. Hamilton 1973, Harmondsworth: Penguin.

—— (400 BCc) *Seventh Letter*, in *Phaedrus and the Seventh and Eighth Letters*, trans. and intr. W. Hamilton 1973, Harmondsworth: Penguin.

—— (395 BC) *Gorgias*, trans. and intr. W. Hamilton, revised edn 1971, Harmondsworth: Penguin.

—— (385 BC) *Meno*, in *Protagoras and Meno*, trans. W.K.C. Guthrie 1956, London: Penguin.

—— (375 BC) *The Republic*, trans. and intr. D. Lee, revised edn 1987, Harmondsworth: Penguin.

Plutarch (100) 'Life of Theseus', in *The Rise and Fall of Athens: Nine Greek Lives by Plutarch*, 1960, trans. and intr. I. Scott-Kilvert, Harmondsworth: Penguin.

Post, E.L. (1936) 'Finite combinatory processes. Formulation 1', in M. Davis (ed.), *The Undecidable: Basic Papers on Undecidable Propositions, Unsolvable Problems and Computable Functions*, 1965, Hewlett, NY: Raven Press.

Poster, M. (1990) *The Mode of Information: Post-structuralism and Social Context*, Cambridge: Polity Press in association with, Basil Blackwell.

Price, S. (1985) 'Delphi and divination', in P.E. Easterling and J.V. Muir (eds), *Greek Religion and Society*, Cambridge: Cambridge University Press.

Quillian, M.R. (1968) 'Semantic memory', in M. Minsky (ed.), *Semantic Information Processing*, Cambridge, MA, and London: MIT Press.

Quine, W.V.O. (1937) 'New foundations for mathematical logic', in W.V.O. Quine, *From a Logical Point of View: Logico-Philosophical Essays*, 1953, Cambridge, MA: Harvard University Press.

Ramsey, F.P. (1923) 'Critical notice of Ludwig Wittgenstein, *Tractatus Logico-philosophicus*', in F.P. Ramsey, *The Foundations of Mathematics and Other Logical Essays*, ed. R.B. Braithwaite 1931, London: Routledge and Kegan Paul.

Ramsey, F.P. (1925) 'Universals', in F.P. Ramsey, *Foundations: Essays in Philosophy, Logic, Mathematics and Economics*, ed. D.H. Mellor 1978, London and Henley: Routledge and Kegan Paul.

—— (1926a) 'The foundations of mathematics', in F.P. Ramsey, *Foundations: Essays in Philosophy, Logic, Mathematics and Economics*, ed. D.H. Mellor 1978, London and Henley: Routledge and Kegan Paul.

—— (1926b) 'Truth and probability', in F.P. Ramsey, *Foundations: Essays in Philosophy, Logic, Mathematics and Economics*, ed. D.H. Mellor 1978, London and Henley: Routledge and Kegan Paul.

—— (1927) 'Facts and propositions', in F.P. Ramsey, *Foundations: Essays in Philosophy, Logic, Mathematics and Economics*, ed. D.H. Mellor 1978, London and Henley: Routledge and Kegan Paul.

Rayward-Smith, V.J. (1986) *A First Course in Computability*, Oxford: Blackwell Scientific.

Report of the Copyright (1952) *Report of the Copyright Committee* (Cmnd 8662), London: HMSO.

Reynolds, L. (1979) 'Legibility studies: their relevance to present-day documentation methods', *Journal of Documentation*, 35: 307–40.

Roberts, N. (1982) 'A search for information man', *Social Science Information Studies*, 2: 93–104.

Roberts, N. and Clarke, D. (1987a) *The Treatment of Information Issues and Concepts in Management and Organizational Literatures* (CRUS Occasional Paper 15; British Library Research and Development Division Report 5951), Sheffield: Consultancy and Research Unit, Department of Information Studies, University of Sheffield.

—— (1987b) *Information Education in Business and Management Schools: A Review from the Perspective of Schools of Librarianship and Information Studies* (CRUS Working Paper 10; British Library Research and Development Division Report 5943), Sheffield: Consultancy and Research Unit, Department of Information Studies, University of Sheffield.

Rouse, R.H. and Rouse, M.H. (1989) 'Wax tablets', *Language and Communication*, 9: 175–91.

Russell, B. (1903) *The Principles of Mathematics*, 2nd edn 1937, London: George Allen & Unwin.

—— (1927) *An Outline of Philosophy*, London: George Allen & Unwin.

Ryan, A. (1988) *Bertrand Russell: A Political Life*, London: Penguin.

Ryle, G. (1949) *The Concept of Mind*, 1988, Harmondsworth: Penguin.

Samarin, W.J. (1969) 'The art of Gbeya insults', *International Journal of American Linguistics*, 35: 323–9.

Sapir, E. (1921) *Language: An Introduction to the Study of Speech*, 1978, London: Granada.

Saussure, F. de (1916) *Course in General Linguistics*, ed. C. Bally and A. Sechehaye with the collaboration of A. Riedlinger, trans. and annotated R. Harris 1983, London: Duckworth.

Schmandt-Besserat, D. (1978) 'The earliest precursor of writing', *Scientific American*, 238, 6: 38–47.

Searle, J.R. (1980) 'Minds, brains and programs', *The Behavioral and Brain Sciences*, 3: 417–57.

Sergot, M. (1988) 'Representing legislation as logic programs', in J.E.

Hayes, D. Michie and J. Richards (eds), *Machine Intelligence 11: Logic and the Acquisition of Knowledge*, Oxford: Clarendon Press.

Shakespeare, W. (1600) *Antony and Cleopatra*, in P. Alexander (ed.), *William Shakespeare: The Complete Works*, 1951, London and Glasgow: Collins, 1155–96.

Shannon, C.E. (1956) 'A universal Turing machine with two internal states', in C.E. Shannon and J. McCarthy (eds), *Automata Studies*, Princeton, NJ: Princeton University Press.

Shannon, C.E. and McCarthy, J. (1956) *Automata Studies*, Princeton, NJ: Princeton University Press.

Shannon, C.E. and Weaver, W. (1949) *The Mathematical Theory of Communication*, Urbana: University of Illinois Press.

Shields, M.W. (1987) *An Introduction to Automata Theory*, Oxford: Blackwell Scientific.

Sloman, A. (1983) 'An overview of some unsolved problems in artificial intelligence', in K. P. Jones (ed.), *Informatics 7: Intelligent Information Retrieval* (Proceedings of a conference held by the Aslib Informatics Group and the Information Retrieval Group of the British Computer Society, Cambridge, 22–23 March 1983), London: Aslib.

Sommerhalder, R. and Van Westrhenen, S.C. (1988) *The Theory of Computability: Programs, Machines, Effectiveness and Feasibility*, Wokingham: Addison-Wesley.

Sperber, D. and Wilson, D. (1986) *Relevance: Communication and Cognition*, Oxford: Basil Blackwell.

Strachey, L. (1918) *Eminent Victorians*, 1986, London: Penguin.

Sturrock, J. (1986) *Structuralism*, London: Paladin Grafton Books.

Turing, A.M. (1937) 'On computable numbers, with an application to the Entscheidungsproblem' (Paper read 12 November 1936), *Proceedings of the London Mathematical Society*, 42: 230–65.

—— (1948) 'Intelligent machinery', in B. Meltzer and D. Michie (eds), *Machine Intelligence 5*, 1969, Edinburgh: Edinburgh University Press. The editors state that this paper was submitted as a report to the National Physical Laboratory but had not been previously published.

—— (1950) 'Computing machinery and intelligence', in A.R. Anderson (ed.), *Minds and Machines*, 1964, Englewood Cliffs, NJ: Prentice-Hall.

Twain, M. (1875) 'Some learned fables for good old boys and girls', in C. Neider (ed.), *The Complete Short Stories of Mark Twain*, 1981, New York: Bantam Books.

—— (1884) *The Adventures of Huckleberry Finn*, 1986, Berkeley and Los Angeles: University of California Press.

Uldall, H.J. (1944) 'Speech and writing', *Acta Linguistica*, 4, 11: 11–16.

Vico, G. (1710) *On the Most Ancient Wisdom of the Italians: Unearthed from the Origins of the Latin Language: Including the Disputation with the Giornale de' Letterati d'Italia*, trans. and intr. L.M. Palmer 1988, Ithaca and London: Cornell University Press.

—— (1725) *The Autobiography of Giambattista Vico*, trans. M.H. Fisch and T.G. Bergin 1944, Ithaca and London: Cornell University Press.

—— (1744) *The New Science of Giabattista Vico*, unabridged translation of the Third Edition (1744) with the addition of 'Practic of the New

Science' by T.G. Bergin and M.H. Fisch 1976, Ithaca and London: Cornell University Press.

Von Strassburg, G. (1215) 'Tristan', in *Tristan. With the Surviving Fragments of the Tristan of Thomas*, trans. and intr. A.T. Hatto 1960, Harmondsworth: Penguin.

Wang, H. (1960) 'Towards mechanical mathematics', *IBM Journal of Research and Develoment*, 4: 2–22.

—— (1974) *From Mathematics to Philosophy*, London: Routledge and Kegan Paul.

Warner, J. (1983) 'Liberalism and Marxism in the work of George Orwell', unpublished D. Phil. thesis, Oxford University.

—— (1984) 'Emperor Hirohito and the English press: the treatment of his state visit to Britain in English national daily newspapers', unpublished M.A. Librarianship thesis, University of Sheffield.

—— (1990) 'Semiotics, information science, documents and computers', *Journal of Documentation*, 46: 16–32.

—— (1993) 'Writing and literary work in copyright: a binational and historical analysis', *Journal of the American Society for Information Science*, 44, 6: 307–21.

Watson, L.E., Gammage, P., Grayshon, M.C., Hockey, S., Jones, R.K. and Watson, D. (1973) 'Sociology and information science', *Journal of Librarianship*, 5: 270–83.

Weizenbaum, J. (1976) *Computer Power and Human Reason: From Judgement to Calculation*, 1984, London and Harmondsworth: Penguin.

Whitehead, A.N. and Russell, B. (1913) *Principia Mathematica to *56*, 2nd edn 1962, Cambridge: Cambridge University Press.

Wilkins, J. (1668) *An Essay towards a Real Character and a Philosophical Language*, London: Royal Society.

Williams, R. (1958) *Culture and Society*, London: Chatto and Windus.

Wilson, P. (1983) *Second-hand Knowledge: An Enquiry into Cognitive Authority* (Contributions in Librarianship and Information Science 44), London and Connecticut: Greenwood Press.

Wittgenstein, L. (1922) *Tractatus Logico-philosophicus*, 1981, London and New York: Routledge and Kegan Paul.

Young, T. (1823) *An Account of some Recent Discoveries in Hieroglyphical Literature and Egyptian Antiquities including the Author's Original Alphabet, as Extended by Mr Champollion, with a Translation of Five Unpublished Greek and Egyptian Manuscripts*, London: John Murray.

Index